# the Glorious Names of GOD

## Mary Foxwell Loeks

**BAKER BOOK HOUSE**
Grand Rapids, Michigan 49506

This special edition is published with permission from the original publisher, Baker Book House Company, 1019 S.E. Wealthy Street, Grand Rapids, MI 49506.

Copyright © 1986 by
Baker Book House Company

ISBN: 0-8010-5629-2

Printed in the United States of America

To **John,**
who suggested the idea
for this book

# Contents

# Join All the Glorious Names

Isaac Watts

John Darwall

1 Join all the glo-rious names Of wis - dom, love, and power,
2 Great Pro-phet of my God, My tongue would bless Thy Name:
3 Je sus, my great High Priest, Of - fered His blood, and died;
4 I love my Shep-herd's voice: His watch-ful eye shall keep
5 My Sav - ior and my Lord, My Con - quer'r and my King,

That ev - er mor - tals knew, That an - gels ev - er
By Thee the joy - ful news Of our sal - va - tion
My guilt - y con - science seeks No sac - ri - fice be -
My wan - d'ring soul a - mong The thou-sands of His
Thy scep - tre and Thy sword, Thy reign - ing grace I

bore: All are too mean to speak His worth, Too
came, The joy - ful news of sins for - giv'n Of
side: His pow'r - ful blood did once a - tone And
sheep: He feeds His flock, He calls their names, His
sing: Thine is the pow'r; be - hold I sit In

mean to set my Sav - ior forth.
hell sub - dued and peace with heav'n.
now it pleads be - fore the throne.
bos - om bears the ten - der lambs.
will - ing bonds be - neath Thy feet. A - men.

# Preface

This is a book of invitations to worship. Each meditation is an attempt to attribute worth to our God by naming one of his names. They are designed to be used in private worship or by those who wish to lead a group in a brief time of focusing on God and who he is.

As I have studied these names, I have been impressed with how many pairs of them stand in stark contrast to each other! God is the Lord and the Servant. He is the Lamb and the Lion, and the Lioness. He is the Shepherd and the Lamb. He is the Alpha and the Omega; the Jehovah and the Abba.

The minute we have the audacity to think we understand God, he brings to mind another name, equally true, but which seems to shatter the mold we have just tried to cram him into. Looking at these contrasting pairs of names is like seeing only the "legs" of a giant parabola! We know they meet and are one, even if we don't quite see how.

11

Name the names of our God with me, and as you name them be full of wonder that our great God has said, "I have called *you* by name, you are mine" (Isa. 43:1b, RSV).

# 1

## Alpha
**Scripture:** Genesis 1:1–2; John 1:1–14

In the beginning God . . . [Gen. 1:1]

In the beginning was the Word, and the Word was with God, and the Word was God. He was with God in the beginning. [John 1:1–2]

"I am the *Alpha* . . . , the First . . . , the Beginning. . . ." [Rev. 22:13]

Time had a beginning. Creation had a beginning. We had a beginning. Civilizations have a beginning. Books have a beginning. All of the endeavors we would undertake have their beginning.

But God? God has no beginning. Before any other beginning began, he was. "Before Abraham was born, I am!" declared Jesus (John 8:58). Why, then, would the eternal God have named himself Alpha, the first letter of the Greek alphabet, the beginning? It must have been because he is the great Beginner of all other

13

beginnings! "Through him all things were made; without him nothing was made that has been made" (John 1:3).

Alpha, God: We lay before you that which we will attempt to begin this day. We acknowledge that without you, all our attempts at beginnings are in vain. We can't see what will result from that which we now begin. Apprehension is mixed with our enthusiasm. We place it before you, Alpha, God, knowing that you see not just the beginning, but the whole.

We worship you, we build our lives upon you, our Alpha God, who is truly without beginning.

> Of the Father's love begotten
> Ere the worlds began to be,
> He is Alpha and Omega,
> He the source, the ending he,
> Of the things that are, that have been,
> And that future years shall see,
> Evermore and evermore!
>
> Christ, to thee, with God the Father,
> And, O Holy Ghost, to thee,
> Hymn and chant and high thanksgiving,
> And unwearied praises be:
> Honor, glory, and dominion,
> And eternal victory,
> Evermore and evermore.

—Aurelius Clemens Prudentius (348–c. 410)

# 2

## The Door

**Scripture:** Exodus 12:7; John 10:1–10

I am *the door*: by me if any man enter in, he shall be saved, and shall go in and out, and find pasture. [John 10:9, KJV]

They were very ordinary doors, set in very ordinary houses. Their uniqueness lay only in the fact that their frames had been freshly painted with lamb's blood.

These doors closed out the cold night air and the turmoil and pain of the outside world. The angel of death was engaged in a terrible mission that night. Relentlessly, one by one, he summoned the first-born in all the other houses. But he would not violate the closed doors framed in lamb's blood. Within these doors were peace and a quiet expectancy that could not be understood by those outside.

Next morning, many walked out through those same bloodframed doors. They left behind their slavery. The open door led them to opportunity and freedom.

O Jesus Christ, we worship you! You are the Door those doors of long ago were pointing toward. You are the Door, and the frame is painted with your blood.

You are the Door which closes out that which would destroy us, providing us peace and safety as we take refuge behind you.

You are the Door which opens up to us opportunity, freedom, and "life . . . to the full."

Today we claim your protection. We claim the abundant life to which you would lead us. We claim the Lamb's blood on your doorframe. We love you, Lord Jesus, our Door.

# 3

## Jesus
**Scripture:** Matthew 1:18–24; Revelation 22:20–21

"She will give birth to a son, and you are to give him the name *Jesus*, because he will save his people from their sins." [Matt. 1:21]

Above his head they placed the written charge against him: THIS IS JESUS, THE KING OF THE JEWS. [Matt. 27:37]

Therefore God exalted him to the highest place
   and gave him the name that is above every
      name,
that at the name of Jesus every knee should bow,
   in heaven and on earth and under the earth,
and every tongue confess that Jesus Christ is
      Lord,
   to the glory of God the Father. [Phil. 2:9–11]

"By faith in the name of Jesus, this man whom you see and know was made strong. It is Jesus' name and the faith that comes through him that has given this complete healing to him, as you can all see." [Acts 3:16]

He who testifies to these things says, "Yes, I am coming soon." Amen. Come, Lord Jesus. The grace of the Lord Jesus be with God's people. Amen. [Rev. 22:21]

**M**any names, when traced to their origin, describe the job or occupation of the one so named: Smith, Taylor (tailor), Baker, Butler, Fisher, Carpenter. The Gospel writer Matthew records a dream in which Joseph was told to name the son his wife-to-be Mary would bear Jesus, because of the job he would do. He would save his people from their sin. Jesus is the Jehovah-Savior.

Sin sometimes comes in a gilded wrapping, but when viewed for what it is, it is never a pretty subject. Sin is ugly. It is a slap in the face of God. It cannot go unpunished.

Greek and Roman mythology is full of tales of how the gods punished mortals for various sins committed against them.

Arachne was a young Greek girl whose pride was her downfall. She thought she could weave more skillfully than the goddess Athena, and challenged the goddess to a competition. As a punishment, Arachne and her descendants were changed forever into the form of spiders.

Sisyphus had the audacity to trick the gods into giving him something he wanted. For his punishment, he was made to push a huge boulder up a steep hill. Every time it almost reached the top, it would slip from his hands and roll back down, and he was made to roll it back up again, and again, and again—eternally.

Tantalus murdered his son in a misguided attempt to make an offering to the gods. The gods punished him by making him stand forever in water up to his neck. But he was never able to quench his thirst, for whenever he bent to drink, the water receded. Above his head hung branches loaded with fruit, but whenever he tried to pick one, the branch bent out of his reach.

You and I have sinned. We deserve eternal punishment, just as did the sinful humans depicted in the Greek myths. But unlike the gods which are creations of human imagination, the real God truly loves the people he made, even though they are sinful. So Jesus came.

Jesus himself wore our pride to the cross. Unlike Arachne, we won't need to wear its consequences throughout eternity.

Jesus himself carried the huge boulder of our sin to the cross—and rolled it away forever.

Jesus freed us from our sin by his death on the cross, and put living Water eternally within our reach.

There is power in the name of Jesus. It is the power to forgive sins and to change lives. The blind man, Bartimaeus, received his sight when he called on the name of Jesus (Mark 10:46–52). Peter and John invoked the power of the name of Jesus, and a lame man began to walk and leap and praise God (Acts 3:1–16). A meeting with the Jesus he had been persecuting completely turned around the life of the man Saul of Tarsus. And there will come a day when every knee in heaven, on earth, or under the earth will bow, acknowledging at last that Jesus Christ is Lord.

I lay my sins on Jesus, the spotless Lamb of God;
He bears them all, and frees us from the accursed
load:
I bring my guilt to Jesus, to wash my crimson stains
White in his blood most precious, 'till not a spot
remains.

—Horatius Bonar, 1843

Today we call your name, Jesus, Anointed One—
set apart before the beginning of time, sent in the
fullness of time, to free us for all time and eternity.

# 4

## The God Who Sees Me
**Scripture:** Genesis 16; 21:8–20

She gave this name to the LORD who spoke to her: "You are *the God who sees me*," for she said, "I have now seen the One who sees me." [Gen. 16:13]

During the construction of the National Cathedral in Washington, D.C., a visitor stopped to watch an elderly stone carver working painstakingly at his craft. The visitor noted that when this particular piece of carving was put in place, it would be next to the wall, where no one could see it.

"Why are you working so hard on something no one will ever see?" asked the amazed onlooker.

"God will see it," replied the carver.

Sometimes it is a little unsettling to realize that ours is a God who is all-seeing! We'd rather put our mistakes and blemishes in the shadows, in a corner, against a wall—anything to get them out of sight. At times we succeed in hiding that which we wish to hide from other people, but we never can hide it from God's penetrating, purifying gaze:

> The eyes of the LORD are everywhere,
>     keeping watch on the wicked and the good. [Prov. 15:3]

But there are other times, when, like Hagar, we marvel with gratitude at the God who sees. The problems we encounter that no one else seems to understand—God sees. The pain we feel—God sees. The tasks we perform for which no one thanks us or pats us on the back—God sees.

> He will not let your foot slip—
>     he who watches over you will not slumber;
> indeed, he who watches over Israel
>     will neither slumber nor sleep.
> The LORD watches over you—
>     the LORD is your shade at your right hand;
> the sun will not harm you by day,
>     nor the moon by night.
> The LORD will keep you from all harm—
>     he will watch over your life;
> The LORD will watch over your coming and going
>     both now and forevermore.
>
> [Ps. 121:3–8]

Seeing God, we praise you for penetrating and purging the dark corners of our sinfulness.

Seeing God, we praise you for protecting and preserving us from harm and danger.

Seeing God, we praise you for feeling even our private pain along with us.
Seeing God, we praise your name!

# 5

## Lord

**Scripture:** Psalm 8; Isaiah 40:3–5

O LORD, our *Lord*, how majestic is your name in all the earth! [Ps. 8:1]

"And the glory of the LORD will be revealed,
and all mankind together will see it.
For the mouth of the LORD has spoken."
[Isa. 40:5]

On his robe and on his thigh he has this name written: . . . LORD OF LORDS. [Rev. 19:16]

"I am the Lord; that is my name!
I will not give my glory to another
or my praise to idols." [Isa. 42:8]

The title *lord* has lost some of its impact in our egalitarian culture. In feudal society, a lord was a man of high rank, perhaps even a king. He might have been the proprietor of a manor, or a man who had mastery in a given field. The relationship of a servant to his lord was a formal, respectful one. The title *lord* demanded unquestioning obedience from the servant.

The disciple Peter's outburst, "Surely not, Lord! . . . I have never eaten anything impure or unclean" (Acts 10:14), was a contradiction in terms. To say "surely not" in response to his Lord's invitation was to deny lordship. That what Peter was asked to do ran counter to the customs and traditions with which he had been brought up was not a consideration.

But before we are too hard on Peter, we need to consider our own responses:

"But, Lord . . ."

"Not me, Lord . . ."

"No, Lord."

"Lord, why?"

Sometimes our outbursts are spoken, sometimes not. Our Lord has every right to say to his disciples and to us, "Why do you call me, 'Lord, Lord,' and do not do what I say?" (Luke 6:46).

The problem with feudal lords was that they were not all-knowing, so they sometimes made unwise demands. Some did not truly love their servants, so they misused the power of their lordship.

We need not fear that kind of abuse of power. The One we call Lord loved us enough to give his own life for us. He is all-knowing and all-wise. The commands he gives us spring from that love and that wisdom and demand our obedience. One servant wrote of this Lord:

> Were the whole realm of nature mine,
> That were a present far too small;
> Love so amazing, so divine,
> Demands my soul, my life, my all.

> —Isaac Watts, 1709

Today, let us respond to the invitation of the psalmist:

> Glorify the LORD with me;
> let us exalt his name together. [Ps. 34:3]

# 6

## Servant
**Scripture:** John 13:1–17; Philippians
2:1–11; Isaiah 42:1

"Here is my *servant,* whom I uphold,
 my chosen one in whom I delight;
I will put my Spirit on him
 and he will bring justice to the nations." [Isa.
  42:1; cf. Matt. 12:18]

Jesus knew that the Father had put all things
under his power, and that he had come from God
and was returning to God; so he got up from the
meal, took off his outer clothing, and wrapped a
towel around his waist. After that, he poured
water into a basin and began to wash his
disciples' feet, drying them with the towel that
was wrapped around him. [John 13:3–5]

Your attitude should be the same as that of
Christ Jesus:

Who, being in very nature God,
 did not consider equality with God something
  to be grasped,

but made himself nothing,
    taking the very nature of a servant,
    being made in human likeness. [Phil. 2:5–7]

The dinner guests all arrived on foot. Open sandals were all that protected their feet from the dusty roads. Customarily, a servant from the host's household would have met them at the door and washed and dried their feet. That nicety had been overlooked this particular night. It was to a borrowed room that this group had come to observe the Passover feast. One of the men seated at the table slipped from his place, stripped down to the short tunic which was all a servant would have worn, and wrapped a towel about himself. He went around the group without a word, kneeling at the feet of each of the men present, and washed and dried them. Until he reached the place of the man called Peter. Undoubtedly all of the men had realized the incongruity of the situation—they probably all felt a little sheepish. Here was the man they called Lord and Teacher performing a most menial task for them! But their sheepishness had rendered them speechless. Except for Peter.

"Not my feet!" Peter protested.

But Jesus was insistent. "Unless I wash you, you have no part with me" (John 3:8).

Who was this guest-turned-servant? He was truly God. But he did not grasp his God-ness. He set it aside and submitted to servanthood.

His was not a conditional submission: I'll submit to you, if you submit to me; or, I'll serve if you'll give me lots of sympathy for doing this miserable job; or,

I'll do it in exchange for a generous supply of credit, attention, and pats on the back.

Most of us don't understand servanthood very well. Jesus laid aside his God-ness to help us understand. Being a servant means considering others better than oneself. It means looking out for the other person's interests and needs first. Being a servant means being obedient. It means attributing all credit and honor to the one served. To truly serve takes nobility of the truest sort.

The One whose name is above every name knelt and washed dirty feet to set an example for us.

> May the mind of Christ my Savior
> Live in me from day to day
> By His love and power controlling
> All I do and say.
>
> May His beauty rest upon me
> As I seek the lost to win.
> And may they forget the channel,
> Seeing only Him.*
>
> —Kate B. Wilkinson (1859–1928)

Today, as an act of worship to God, let us try to find a practical way to follow Christ's example.

---

*Taken from "May the Mind of Christ My Savior," and used by permission of the executors of the estate of the Reverend A. C. Barham Gould.

# 7

## The Way

**Scripture:** John 14:1–6; Hebrews
10:19–25; Psalm 1

... the blood of Jesus, ... a new and living way
opened for us ... [Heb. 10:19b–20a]

"I am *the way*. ... No one comes to the Father
except through me." [John 14:6]

The lone mountain climber, partway up
Mount Fuji, reached a fork in the trail. One of the
trails was marked by a sign, its message painted boldly
and clearly. This was the way the climber chose to
follow. The mountain climber was a scholar, conver-
sant in a number of classical and modern languages.
But he didn't know Japanese and thus couldn't read
the message on that boldly painted sign. The message
read: "Danger! This way should be attempted only
by the most skilled and experienced climbers." Having taken the wrong way, this climber fell and lost
his life.

Signs clutter our streets and highways. Sometimes they amuse us, sometimes they disgust us, sometimes they provide useful information. The intent of the one who places a sign is that we will pursue a certain prescribed course of action or follow in a certain way.

Because of sin, man has lost his way. He is without direction or purpose, with no hope of finding reconciliation with the Father. The bridge is out. There is no crossing the deep chasm created by sin.

But Jesus, like a bold signpost, declares authoritatively, "I am the way. . . . No one comes to the Father except through me." Then Jesus literally, physically, became the way. His death on our behalf provided the bridge to cross the chasm. It made possible our reconciliation with the Father.

There are those who resent the exclusiveness Jesus implies: "No one comes . . . except through me." "God isn't being fair," they say. "There must be another way for those who mean well, and try hard, but haven't encountered *the* Way." If that were true, if there had been any other way, then the Father God's act of sending his dearly loved Son to shoulder the world's sin as he died on the cross was the most hideously absurd act ever committed.

Unlike the sign on Mount Fuji, Jesus' message, "I am the Way," is clear and can be read by all. But the consequence of taking a wrong way, even with the best of intentions, is certain death.

The Way is not always smoothly paved. Following the Way is not always easy. It is not always fun. It does not always follow the most scenic route. Sometimes our feet will hurt; sometimes we will be bonetired. Sometimes we will be lonely. At other times,

31

the rudeness of other travelers along the way will irritate us. Sometimes we will wish we could turn back; we may even wonder at times if we have made a mistake.

But the Way is sure, and leads to a sure end—eternal life through Jesus Christ, our Lord, our living Way.

# 8

## The Truth

**Scripture:** Psalm 25:4–5, 8–9; John 8:31–32

Jesus answered, "I am . . . *the truth*. . . . No one comes to the Father except through me." [John 14:6]

Jesus said, "If you hold to my teaching, you are really my disciples. Then you will know the truth, and the truth will set you free." [John 8:31–32]

Goaded by his fickle subjects, Pontius Pilate allowed the Truth to slip through his fingers, unnamed and unclaimed. He asked the right question, but he would not allow himself to see that the answer stood right before him.

Acknowledging the Truth would not have been politically expedient for Pontius Pilate. Indeed, pursuing truth can be costly, inconvenient, uncomfortable, even dangerous. Many of us know people who have lost friends, jobs, material things, or their lives because they pursued truth.

But Pilate was mistaken if he really thought he could "wash his hands" of his responsibility to deal with the Truth (Matt. 27:24). Exposure to the Truth demands a response. For the One who said, "I am . . . the truth" went on to say, "No one comes to the Father except through me." By choosing the politically expedient way, Pilate lost his opportunity to find the Way and the Truth.

Truth is a searching spotlight, leaving for one intent on pursuing evil no shadows in which to hide. But for one seeking to follow God, this same spotlight is a welcome revealer of the obstacles over which he might otherwise have stumbled.

For us who would belong to God, following the Truth is not optional. The apostle Paul urges us to think on "whatsoever things are true . . ." (Phil. 4:8, KJV). But like pure water and pure air around us, pure truth is hard to come by. The clarity of truth may be shadowed by unbelief, impure motives, and careless inattention. The impact of truth without love is like that of surgery on one whose body is incapable of healing. The impact of truth without wisdom is like that of light shining on the path of a blind man.

The beauty of Jesus, our Truth, is that he is the God of love as well as the God of wisdom. Jesus is God's true expression of himself.

Jesus Christ, our Truth, we worship you, and we want you to have an impact on our lives this day.

# 9

## The Life
**Scripture:** John 11:1–44

"I am . . . *the life*. No one comes to the Father except through me." [John 14:6]

Jesus said to her, "I am the resurrection and the life. He who believes in me will live, even though he dies; and whoever lives and believes in me will never die." [John 11:25]

In the nine long months of waiting, we could see the ever-expanding belly—an indication of life about to be. We could feel, even sometimes see, the baby's movements (surely this one will be a gymnast!). This too was an indication of life about to be. Aided by a stethoscope we could sometimes hear the baby's heartbeat. Still more indication of life about to be. And we waited.

Finally the day arrives, the little girl emerges, the cord is clamped. Several seconds pass, each seeming like an eternity. Then we hear it, the first wail of this newborn baby! This is the cry that declares for all to hear, "I am breathing on my own. I am receiving the life you have hoped for, prayed for, and labored for." The gift of life demands a response.

The commencement of eternal life is also signaled by a birth, sometimes referred to as the second birth. Jesus told Nicodemus that "unless one is born anew, he cannot see the kingdom of God" (John 3:3, RSV). God himself, in the person of Jesus, has experienced indescribably excruciating labor to make our new birth possible. Others may have hoped and prayed for it to happen. Perhaps it is inevitable, but there must indeed come a time of affirmation, the baby's first wail: "Yes, I am receiving this life. Yes, I acknowledge the implications. I realize, as did the apostle Paul, that 'I have been crucified with Christ and I no longer live, but Christ lives in me' " (Gal. 2:20a).

Naming Jesus Life gets at the very essence of what Christianity is all about. But in order to be Life for us, he first had to be our death. And because of who he was, God-man, his very real death could be followed by a very real coming alive, a resurrection.

Jesus felt pain at the death of his friend, Lazarus. He wept. But the One who named himself both the Resurrection and the Life was able to lock this pain of death into that small sliver of eternity known as time.

Jesus Christ, because you first named yourself Resurrection and Life, we are able to call you by these names today. In doing so, we strain to catch a glimpse of what that abundant life, lived beyond time, will mean.

Thou only art true Life,
To know Thee is to live
The more abundant life
That earth can never give:
O risen Lord! We live in Thee,
And Thou in us eternally.*

—E. Margaret Clarkson

*Taken from the hymn "We Come, O Christ, to Thee" by E. Margaret
Clarkson. © by Inter-Varsity Christian Fellowship of the USA and used
by permission of InterVarsity Press, Downers Grove, IL 60515.

# 10

## Teacher

**Scripture:** Psalm 25:4–5, 8–9, 12; Psalm 31:8; Psalm 119:33; Matthew 5:2; John 14:26

I will instruct you and teach you in the way you
   should go;
   I will counsel you and watch over you. [Ps.
   32:8]

And he will be called Wonderful Counselor. . . .
[Isa. 9:6]

"Rabbi, we know you are a *teacher* who has
come from God." [John 3:2]

". . . for the Holy Spirit will teach you. . . ."
[Luke 12:12]

We have all known teachers. What qualities come to mind as we recall the best teachers we have known? May these qualities also be attributed to the greatest of all teachers, God himself?

*A teacher who will bend down and listen.* What a gift we have in such a teacher! The psalmist is confident that he will be heard, that God will "incline His ear" and hear what he has to say. "I have called upon thee, for thou wilt hear me, O God: incline thine ear unto me, and hear my speech" (Ps. 17:6, KJV).

*A teacher who knows his subject matter.* Our teacher is God himself. Who could better show us the Father and teach us his way? We are promised,

> When . . . the Spirit of truth comes, he will guide you into all truth. (John 16:13)

> But the Counselor, the Holy Spirit, whom the Father will send in my [Jesus'] name, will teach you all things. (John 14:26)

> He [the Spirit] will not speak on his own; he will speak only what he hears. . . . [He] will take from what is mine and make it known to you. (John 16:13, 15)

Indeed, our teacher knows his subject matter.

*A teacher who knows his students.* How well our Teacher knows us! "He lives with you and will be in you" (John 14:17). As the psalmist observed,

> O LORD, you have searched me
>   and you know me.
> You know when I sit and when I rise;
>   you perceive my thoughts from afar.
> You discern my going out and my lying down;
>   you are familiar with all my ways.
> Before a word is on my tongue
>   you know it completely, O LORD.

> You hem me in—behind and before;
>   you have laid your hand upon me. [Ps. 139:1–5]

It is both uncomfortable and comforting to be taught by One who knows us like this!

*A teacher who is able to individualize his instruction, who will challenge without becoming either frustrating or boring!* The apostle Paul assures us that "God keeps faith, and he will not allow you to be tested above your powers, but when the test comes he will at the same time provide a way out, by enabling you to sustain it" (1 Cor. 10:13, NEB). Another student wrote,

> How sweet are your words to my taste,
>   sweeter than honey to my mouth!
> I gain understanding from your precepts;
>   therefore I hate every wrong path. [Ps. 119:103–4]

*A teacher who is an effective and ready counselor.* The advice of our all-wise, all-knowing Teacher is the best and can be relied upon without hesitation. The prophet Isaiah called him Wonderful Counselor.

*A teacher who helps us meet our goals.* We have a teacher who wills for us to walk or "keep in step" (Gal. 5:25) with him. And we can be certain he will carry to completion the good work he has begun in our lives (Phil. 1:6).

Teacher, Counselor, Friend, how can we thank you? We are grateful that you receive the feeble attempts at thanks that we offer today, and that you understand our hearts. May our thanks take the form of increased willingness to be shaped and taught by you and increased obedience to what you have already taught us.

# 11

## The Root, the Vine, the Branch, and the Cup
**Scripture:** John 15:1–16

"I, Jesus, have sent my angel to give you this testimony for the churches. I am *the Root* and the Offspring of David. . . ." [Rev. 22:16]

". . . the Root of David has triumphed. He is able to open the scroll and its seven seals." [Rev. 5:5]

If some of the branches have been broken off, and you, though a wild olive shoot, have been grafted in among the others and now share in the nourishing sap from the olive root, do not boast over those branches. If you do, consider this: You do not support the root, but the root supports you. [Rom. 11:17–18]

"I am the true *vine.* . . . Remain in me, and I will remain in you. No branch can bear fruit by itself; it must remain in the vine." [John 15:1, 4]

"I am the vine; you are the branches." [John 15:5a]

"Here is the man whose name is *the Branch*.
. . ." [Zech. 6:12]

A shoot will come up from the stump of Jesse;
    from his roots a Branch will bear fruit.
The Spirit of the LORD will rest on him—
    the Spirit of wisdom and understanding. . . .
      [Isa. 11:1–2a]

Then he took *the cup*, gave thanks and offered it
to them, saying, "Drink from it, all of you. This
is my blood of the covenant, which is poured out
for many for the forgiveness of sins." [Matt.
26:27–28]

The Root, the Vine, the Branch, and the
cup: named in one sentence, they seem almost a contradiction! One might wish the writers of Scripture
had consulted one another, instead of muddling their
metaphors. But on further reflection, these terms are
neither contradictory nor muddled! All four point to
what Jesus has done for us.

Unless it is planted in good soil, a vine will soon
wither away. The soil in which this vine is planted
is rich with the nutrients of the love of God. The
apostle Paul prayed: "May your roots go down deep
into the soil of God's marvelous love" (Eph. 3:17b,
LB).

The root of the vine is not usually visible, but the
life of the plant depends on it. It is through the root,
firmly fixed in the soil, that moisture and nutrients
are drawn into the rest of the plant. The deeper into
the soil the root goes, the better able the plant is to
bear fruit in times of drought. Deep roots make the
plant less likely to break in a storm or high wind.

The plant springs up through the soil from the root. Jesus could therefore truly be the Root of David, since he was David's Creator as well as David's offspring or Branch. The rest of the plant does not support the root, but the root is the support system for the rest of the plant (Rom. 11:18). Jesus is truly our support system.

And Jesus named himself the Vine. It is to the Vine that the branches must be directly connected, or they will die. After they are brought up through the root, nutrients and moisture are then brought to the branches through the vine. For a branch to be in close proximity to the vine is not enough—just as attending a church or being in a family where others are believers is not enough. The branches must belong to the plant itself. Jesus, the Vine, is our source of living Water and nourishment.

Jesus is "the man whose name is the Branch" (Zech. 6:12). Jesse's tree, the once powerful kingdom of Israel, has been cut down, and compared to what it once was, only a stump is left (Isa. 11:1). But from this stump grows a living Branch, Jesus Christ himself. The purpose of the branch is to bear fruit. The fruit given by the man whose name is the Branch had a very special function.

At the last supper Jesus had with his disciples before he died, he took a cup filled with wine, fruit of the vine, and gave it to them. "Drink from it, all of you. This is my blood of the covenant, which is poured out for many for the forgiveness of sins" (Matt. 26:27b–28).

Jesus—the Branch, the Vine, and the Root springing from the soil of God's love—produced fruit that he poured out on our behalf!

44

Jesus Christ! You are all we need. We love you. Help us, your fellow branches, to bear fruit as we partake of the life of the Vine.

# 12

## Eternal God

**Scripture:** Deuteronomy 33:26–29;
Romans 1:20

"The *eternal God* is your refuge,
   and underneath are the everlasting arms."
   [Deut. 33:27]

Now to the King eternal, immortal, invisible, the only God, be honor and glory for ever and ever. Amen. [1 Tim. 1:17]

Fettered by time as we are, it is hard for us to imagine what the word *eternal* means. People are born and they die. We light a match to start a fire, and when the wood is consumed, it extinguishes itself. Tasks are begun and they are completed. A day begins with the sun's apparent rising and ends when the sun appears to set. We hang a new calendar on the wall when a year begins and take it down at year end. What is it never to have begun and never to end?

Who is the eternal God? What does eternity mean, anyway?

A simple math problem brings to mind one picture of eternity: The problem is to divide three into one. Now there is a long math problem! Infinitely, eternally long! In fact, if someone starts to work that problem today, he will never complete it, even if he keeps working through all eternity! Our mathematician will simply have to decide when to go on to other things. For no matter how many times the three is divided into the one, the one is never completely used up.

The eternal One who is our God has made all his resources available for us to draw on. Even when we are released from the bondage of time, we can keep drawing from the eternal One strength, grace, wisdom—all that we need, throughout all of eternity. The supply will never be exhausted.

Infinite, eternal One! Unwittingly we limit you with our finity and short-sightedness. Help us to see more clearly what it means to draw on your infinite, eternal resources. Help us as we live our lives to be mindful that you have made a way for us to share eternity with you.

Infinite, eternal One! Receive our deep gratitude this day.

# 13

## The Morning Star
**Scripture:** John 1:4–9; 3:19–21

"I, Jesus, have sent my angel to give you this testimony for the churches. I am . . . the bright *Morning Star*." [Rev. 22:16]

"To him who overcomes and does my will to the end, I will give authority over the nations. . . . I will also give him the morning star." [Rev. 2:26, 28]

"I see him, but not now;
  I behold him, but not near.
A star will come out of Jacob;
  a scepter will rise out of Israel." [Num. 24:17]

What is a star? Stars are not the mysteries they once were. Thanks to modern science, we can understand their composition, how far away they are, and how large they are with much more clarity than did our ancestors.

What is a star? A star is a source of light. That light comes from the burning up of its very essence.

It is not reflected light, such as comes to us from the moon and planets.

Perhaps understanding these two types of light can help us to understand Jesus' two seemingly paradoxical statements, "I am the light of the world" and "you are the light of the world." Like a bright and burning ball of fire, Jesus is our source of light. As we reflect his light, we, too, can be light to our world.

To be light, a light source must spend itself. It must literally use itself up. It is difficult for us to fathom what that means for a star, because the "using up" takes place over millions or perhaps billions of years. But consider a burning candle.* Even as we watch it give light for us, we can see that the candle is being used up, spent.

How like our Lord! In order to be light for us, he literally spent himself.

> O Splendor of God's glory bright,
>    From light eternal bringing light,
> Thou Light of light, light's living Spring
>    True Day, all days illumining;
>
> Come, very Sun of heaven's love,
>    In lasting radiance from above,
> And pour the Holy Spirit's ray
>    On all we think or do today.
>
> Dawn's glory gilds the earth and skies,
>    Let him, our perfect Morn, arise,
> The Word in God the Father one,
>    The Father imaged in the Son.
>
> —Ambrose of Milan (340–397)

*If you are using this meditation with a group, you might like to have a candle burning while you talk.

Jesus, our bright Morning Star! Forgive us for taking for granted what it cost you to be light for us.

Jesus, our bright Morning Star! Help us this day to be clearer reflectors of your light, so that we, too, may "shine like stars in the universe as [we] hold out the word of life" (Phil. 2:15b–16a).

# 14

## Rock

**Scripture:** Matthew 7:24–27; Ephesians
2:19–22; 1 Peter 2:6–8

I love you, O LORD, my strength.

The LORD is my *rock*, my fortress and my
    deliverer;
  my God is my rock, in whom I take refuge.
He is my shield and the horn of my salvation,
  my stronghold.

For who is God besides the LORD?
  And who is the Rock except our God?

The LORD lives! Praise be to my Rock!
  Exalted be God my Savior! [Ps. 18:1–2, 31, 46]

He lifted me out of the slimy pit,
  out of the mud and mire;
he set my feet on a rock
  and gave me a firm place to stand. [Ps. 40:2]

Have you ever considered how truly desperate Jacob must have been to choose a rock for a pillow? A rock is hardly a comfortable place to sit for a long time, let alone to sleep on all night. A prolonged or abrupt encounter with a rock is not what most of us would consider comfortable—it can indeed be downright painful!

But there is a big difference between comfortable and comforting. A rock is a secure place on which to build. Unlike the house built on shifting sand, the house built on the rock withstood the ravages of rain and flood (Matt. 7:24).

A rock is a safe place on which to stand after one has been slipping and sliding about in quicksand (Ps. 40:2). A large rock is secure, fixed, and unmovable. It represents constancy and permanence, something to which to grab hold when everything else about us seems to be changing.

A rock can be a shelter under which to take refuge. It can provide shade from a merciless sun or spare one from the full fury of a driving rain.

An abrupt encounter with a rock cannot be ignored. We cannot pretend it isn't there, especially if the encounter has been painful. Jacob slept with a rock for a pillow. He dreamed and afterward awoke with an awareness of the presence of the Lord. He made a solemn vow as his response (Gen. 28:10–22). In the parable of the tenants (Mark 12:1–12), the visit of the owner's beloved son could not be ignored. The response of the tenants was to reject and kill the owner's son. As Jesus concluded his parable he quoted Scripture:

"The stone the builders rejected
  has become the capstone;

the Lord has done this,
and it is marvelous in our eyes." [Mark 12:10–11]

The same stone will be tripped over by some and used as a firm place to stand by others (Isa. 8:14; 28:16).

Jesus Christ is my rock. He is my refuge, my foundation, my resting place, and my security in the midst of turmoil. The reality of who he is, and what he has done, looms large in front of me and cannot be ignored. Today, my encounter with the Rock demands a response:

May the words of my mouth and the meditation of
    my heart
  be pleasing in your sight,
O LORD, my Rock and my Redeemer. [Ps. 19:14]

# 15

## Holy Spirit
**Scripture:** John 14:15–27

. . . and the Spirit of God was hovering over the waters. [Gen. 1:2b]

"God is spirit, and his worshipers must worship in spirit and in truth." [John 4:24]

"But the Counselor, the *Holy Spirit*, whom the Father will send in my [Jesus'] name, will teach you all things and will remind you of everything I have said to you." [John 14:26]

Don't you know that you youselves are God's temple and that God's Spirit lives in you? [1 Cor. 3:16]

We do not know what we ought to pray for, but the Spirit himself intercedes for us with groans that words cannot express. And he who searches our hearts knows the mind of the Spirit, because the Spirit intercedes for the saints in accordance with God's will. [Rom. 8:26b–27]

Where can I go from your Spirit?
  Where can I flee from your presence?

If I go up to the heavens, you are there;
if I make my bed in the depths, you are there.
[Ps. 139:7–8]

Some of us can remember attempting to make an international telephone call before the days of communications satellites. We marvel at the ease with which someone in the United States today can pick up his own telephone, punch a series of numerals, and in seconds be talking with a person in Tokyo, Nairobi, or Paris. The voice is as easily heard as that of a neighbor down the street.

But even with satellites, there are times when all the circuits are in use and the caller must wait. There are times when no one answers at the other end. There are times when we hear a busy signal. There are times when all we reach is a recording, asking us to leave a name and number after the "beep." As wonderful as satellite telecommunication is, it doesn't begin to compare with the communication system available for an earth-child with his heavenly Father.

A four-year-old girl asked, "Can God really hear everyone who is praying?"

"Yes, he can," she was told.

"Even if a lot of people all over the world are praying at once?"

"He hears them all," was the reply.

"God must wear an awfully big shirt," reflected the child, after a pause.

Even we who are older than four are full of wonder as we think about prayer. It is because God is Spirit, and not bound to a shirt of any size, that prayer is possible. Because God is Spirit, he is always there, the line is never busy, we never get a recording, and we never have to wait.

Often we don't know what to say, or what to ask, or even how to ask. God, the Holy Spirit, conveys the message that we would have given if we could.

Because God is Spirit, he can be simultaneously with us and with people who are dear to us but far away. We have a link to our distant loved ones that those without God, the Spirit, cannot comprehend.

Because God is Spirit, there isn't any place we can go where he isn't. It would be futile to try to hide from him or to run away from him.

Because of the function of God the Spirit, he is not the person of the Godhead that many of us focus on in our prayers and thoughts of God. When we look through a clear, clean window, we don't usually think about the window. We tend to focus on, and think about, what we see through the window. The Holy Spirit is much like that window. Because he is there, we are able to see the Father and the Son. How much and how clearly would we see if the window weren't there?

> Come, O Creator Spirit blest,
> And in our hearts take up thy rest;
> Spirit of grace with heavenly aid
> Come to the souls whom thou hast made.
>
> Show us the Father, Holy One,
> Help us to know th' Eternal Son;
> Spirit Divine, for evermore
> Thee will we trust and thee adore.

—Anonymous, tenth century (Latin)
Trans. George Rawson (1807–1889)

O, Holy Spirit, breath of God! You who are the great Communicator and Illuminator! We worship you today.

# 16

## Living Water
**Scripture:** John 4; Isaiah 55

"Come, all you who are thirsty,
  come to the waters;
and you who have no money,
  come. . . ." [Isa. 55:1a]

Then Jesus declared, ". . . he who believes in me
will never be thirsty." [John 6:35]

. . . wash me, and I will be whiter than snow.
[Ps. 51:7b]

"When you pass through the waters,
  I will be with you;
and when you pass through the rivers,
  they will not sweep over you." [Isa. 43:2a]

Jesus answered her, "If you knew the gift of God
and who it is that asks you for a drink, you
would have asked him and he would have given
you *living water.*" [John 4:10]

We might value water more if we had to

carry it in jars from the edge of town, bearing on our shoulders all the water our household needed each day! But even we who take our abundant water supply for granted can attest to the fact that after several hours of physical exertion on a hot day, nothing quenches thirst like a glass of cold water, no matter what the beverage advertisers would have us think.

Another luxury that not all peoples of all cultures have been able to enjoy is that of frequent bathing—the opportunity to become clean! What a gift it is to be able to wash.

How vital water is for all that grows on the earth—trees, plants, flowers, grass, fruits, vegetables, grains. They all would die if it were not for water.

"The rain and the snow
  come down from heaven,
and do not return to it
  without watering the earth
and making it bud and flourish,
  so that it yields seed for the sower and bread for
    the eater." [Isa. 55:10]

And consider the power of moving water. It alters and erodes riverbanks and shorelines. Sometimes the energy from falling water has been harnessed to provide electricity for entire communities.

Buoyancy—we are sometimes inclined to forget this property of water. A good swimming instructor frequently tells his students: "Swim *through* the water; don't struggle so hard to get above it. The water itself will hold you up if you let it."

Where water is abundant, people have found ways to transport themselves and their goods through it. And children of all ages have enjoyed playing in water.

Jesus, our living Water, forgive us. We have fought and struggled, trying to hold ourselves up in our own strength. We fail to appropriate the fact that, as we rest in you, our living Water, you are with us and are holding us up. Sometimes we have gone about thirsty, dirty, parched, and powerless. You have put living Water at our disposal, but we have sat beside our empty pails, either ignorant of or afraid of the implications of living Water. We can identify with Jill, a character in one of C. S. Lewis's chronicles of Narnia:

'Are you not thirsty?' said the Lion.

'I'm *dying* of thirst,' said Jill.

'Then drink,' said the Lion.

'May I—could I—would you mind going away while I do?' said Jill.

The Lion answered this only by a look and a very low growl . . .

'I daren't come and drink,' said Jill.

'Then you will die of thirst,' said the Lion.

'O dear!' said Jill, coming another step nearer. 'I suppose I must go and look for another stream then.'

'There is no other stream,' said the Lion.*

Jesus Christ, our living Water, we thank you that you yourself are what we need, and all we need, to quench our souls' thirst. We are grateful for the cleansing that you alone can provide us. We are awed at the power available to us.

> The Lord is our strength and song.
> He is become our salvation.

*C. S. Lewis, *The Silver Chair* (New York: Macmillan, 1953), chap. 2, pp. 16–17.

> Today, with joy, we will draw water
> From the wells of salvation,

and we will give thanks to You, our only source of living Water (paraphrase, Isa. 12:2–3).

# 17

## The Gentle Whisper

**Scripture:** 1 Kings 19:9–18; 1 Samuel 3:2–10

"... the LORD is about to pass by. ..." And after the fire came a *gentle whisper.* [1 Kings 19:11, 12]

Enter: one of God's faithful servants. God has only recently used him in a mighty and powerful way. But now this servant of the Lord is feeling alone, discouraged, and afraid.

The message comes: "Go out and stand on the mountain in the presence of the LORD, for the LORD is about to pass by" (1 Kings 19:11).

What must God's servant have felt and thought? Perhaps some skepticism. Surely some amazement. What will it sound like when the mighty Yahweh, Creator of the universe, the one who had poured fire from heaven to consume the water-drenched sacrifice offered by his servant—what will it sound like when this Lord passes by?

Act I: A great and powerful wind rages and roars, tearing mountains apart and splitting huge rocks in two. Is the Lord God in the howling of the wind?*

Act II: Rumble, rumble! The earth itself, once so firm and solid, now begins to shake and tremble. To the helpless, uncertain onlooker, even seconds seem eternities. Is God speaking in the midst of the earth's rumbles?

Act III: Hear now a crackling, spitting fire, blazing and consuming all in its path. Is this the sound of the Lord God passing by?

Act IV: This stands in dramatic contrast to what has just transpired. Peaceful stillness settles over the scene. Listen! Do you hear the gentle whisper? *The Lord God is passing by!* His servant hears and is encouraged.

O God, our Father—sometimes the clamor with which we are surrounded all but drowns out your gentle whisper. Help us to become better listeners. We would claim the prayer of the child Samuel: "Speak, for your servant is listening" (1 Sam. 3:10).

---

*If you are using this with a group, you can provide a few simple sound effects. (Hide objects behind podium or in a paper grocery sack.) For rocks breaking in the wind—hit two wooden blocks together. For the earthquake—place several wooden blocks in shoe box and shake shoe box from side to side. For fire—wrinkle a piece of waxed paper.

# 18

## Last Adam

**Scripture:** Genesis 2:7; Genesis 3;
1 Corinthians 15:20–25, 45–47

The LORD God formed the man from the dust of
the ground and breathed into his nostrils the
breath of life, and the man became a living being.
[Gen. 2:7]

For as in Adam all die, so in Christ all will be
made alive. [1 Cor. 15:22]

So it is written: "The first man Adam became a
living being"; the *last Adam*, a life-giving spirit.
[1 Cor. 15:45]

I t had been an adam* who introduced sin
into the world. An adam cut the chasm that separated
the holy God from the creatures who were his image-
bearers.

*Adam is the Hebrew word for man and may be derived from *ada-
mah*, the Hebrew for ground.

So it had to be an adam, a son of Adam, who would build the bridge to cross that chasm of eternal death. And it had to be an adam who was perfect and without sin. We cannot fully comprehend what had to happen. God himself became adam. The eternal God became a human embryo and locked himself inside a woman's uterus for nine months. He was born in a barn, and his first bed was a box full of animal feed.

The infant "last Adam" must surely have cried when he was hungry or wet.

As an adult, the last Adam wept when his good friend, Lazarus, died.

After one exhausting day, he fell asleep in the boat of his fisherman friends.

He was so furious that a place of worship had been desecrated and corrupted that he made a whip and literally drove away those who were responsible.

He enjoyed relaxing at the home of his friends, Mary, Martha, and Lazarus.

The devil himself tried every one of his tricks on the last Adam, attempting in vain to find a vulnerable area.

The last Adam submitted to the most humiliating of deaths—as a criminal, on a cross. He experienced something no other adam needs to experience—total separation from the Father God.

> All praise to thee, Eternal Lord,
> Clothed in a garb of flesh and blood;
> Choosing a manger for thy throne,
> While worlds on worlds are thine alone.
>
> —Martin Luther, 1524

Accept our worship, eternal Lord, you who became for us the last Adam.

65

# 19

## Redeemer
**Scripture:** Job 19:25–27; Isaiah 44:6–8

Our *Redeemer*—the LORD Almighty is his
     name—
   is the Holy One of Israel. [Isa. 47:4]

"I know that my Redeemer lives,
   and that in the end he will stand upon the
   earth." [Job 19:25]

There is a story that some of us heard as
children. A young boy made for himself a beautiful
little sailboat, sanding, painting, and gluing each of
its parts with great care. It became his favorite pos-
session, and almost daily he went to sail it on the
river near his home. One day a storm came up suddenly, the string on the boat broke, and the boat got
away from him. He spent many days searching for
the boat along the banks of the river, and he began to
fear that he would never see it again.

Months later, his grandfather took him to town,

and as they were poking around in a second-hand shop, the boy spotted a familiar-looking boat, high on one of the shelves, with a price tag attached to it.

"Let me see that boat," he cried. "I think that's the boat I made."

The shopkeeper obligingly took the boat from the shelf.

"See! These are my initials! I carved them in the bottom! This *is* my boat."

"I'm sorry, son. I bought that boat from the man who brought it into the shop. If you want the boat, you'll have to pay for it."

Sadly the boy left the shop. For the next few weeks he worked hard doing every odd job anyone would give him, carefully saving every penny.

At last he had the required amount of money. He went back to the shop and redeemed for himself the boat he had made.

The seeming injustice of having to pay for something that was one's own in the first place rankles a little. But that is the essence of what it means to redeem.

Christ our Creator made us and stamped us with his own image. Then we became separated from him.

Christ our Redeemer bought back the right to own us by paying a price so awful we cannot comprehend it.

Creator, Redeemer God—you have twice the right to own us. You hold our purchase agreement, signed in your blood. Yet some of us, fools that we are, keep trying to snatch back ownership for ourselves.

Give us just a glimpse, today, of what it cost you to redeem us. Receive our bodies as living sacrifices.

Receive the words of our mouths and the thoughts of our hearts.

> I will sing of my Redeemer
> And his wondrous love to me;
> On the cruel cross he suffered
> From the curse to set me free.
>
> Sing, oh sing, of my Redeemer
> With his blood he purchased me.
> On the cross he sealed my pardon,
> Paid the debt and made me free.

—Philip P. Bliss, 1878

# 20

## Merciful God
**Scripture:** Exodus 25:10–22; Ephesians 2:1–5

". . . I am *merciful*," declares the LORD,
  "I will not be angry forever." [Jer. 3:12b]

". . . your Father is *merciful*." [Luke 6:36b]

"God, have mercy on me, a sinner." [Luke 18:13]

But because of his great love for us, God, who is rich in mercy, made us alive with Christ even when we were dead in transgressions—it is by grace you have been saved. [Eph. 2:4–5]

I will sing of the mercies of the LORD for ever: with my mouth will I make known thy faithfulness to all generations. [Ps. 89:1, KJV]

For God's mercy to hold any meaning for us, we must first begin to understand the intensity of God's holiness and the immensity of man's sin. The

69

depth of mercy is in direct relation to the gravity of the wrong.

Sometimes we think of mercy as a rug under which to scoot dirt, or as a frosting to fill and cover that section of the cake which fell. But mercy is more than the superficial covering or overlooking of a wrong. Such a notion makes a mockery of God's holiness. Mercy deals with the wrong itself.

In the Book of Exodus we have recorded for us the careful and detailed instructions God gave the Israelites for building the tabernacle. This was to be their place of worship. In the tabernacle was to be the ark of the covenant, which represented the presence of the holy God. The ark was to be a box, covered inside and out with gold. The box was to be made with two rings on each side, through which gold-covered poles were to be placed. No one, under any circumstances, was to touch the ark itself. In it were placed the tablets on which were inscribed the Ten Commandments, representing the law of God. A gold cover with two cherubim "of hammered gold" was placed on top of the ark. This cover has sometimes been called the mercy seat. The ark with this covering was placed behind a curtain. Only the high priest was allowed to enter that Most Holy Place, and he only once a year on the Day of Atonement. The Israelites had before them a demonstration of God's promise that his mercy would cover his law, which they were unable to keep. They could partake of that mercy, but since the wrong had not yet been made right, their participation had to be from a distance.

At the moment of Jesus' death, the curtain, which for so many years had separated the ark and its mercy seat from view, was ripped from top to bottom. Justice had been done. God himself had paid dearly to right sin's wrongs. The torn curtain stated dramatically that now God's mercy could be available to all who would receive it. Now his mercy was accessible in a way it never had been before.

> Let us wonder;
>    grace and justice join,
>    and point to mercy's store;
> When through grace in Christ our trust is,
> Justice smiles and asks no more.
> He who washed us with his blood,
> Has secured our way to God.
>
> —John Newton, 1774

Merciful God, we confess before you that we have sinned, even this very day. You have not ignored our sin, even though we have a tendency to do so. You have not glossed over it, even though we try to do that as well. You have paid dearly that we might receive mercy instead of the justice we deserve.

> Let us praise, and join the chorus
> Of the saints enthroned on high;
> Here they trusted him before us,
> Now their praises fill the sky:
> "Thou hast washed us with thy blood;
> Thou art worthy, Lamb of God!" Amen.
>
> —John Newton, 1774

# 21

## *Like an Eagle*

**Scripture:** Deuteronomy 32:9–14;
Exodus 19:4; Isaiah 40:28–31

[The Lord] shielded him and cared for him;
   he guarded him as the apple of his eye,
*like an eagle* that stirs up its nest
   and hovers over its young,
that spreads its wings to catch them
   and carries them on its pinions.
The Lord alone led him. . . . [Deut. 32:10b–12a]

"You yourselves have seen what I did to Egypt,
and how I carried you on eagles' wings and
brought you to myself." [Exod. 19:4]

But those who hope in the Lord
   will renew their strength.
They will soar on wings like eagles. . . . [Isa.
    40:31a]

The eagle is one of the largest and most
powerful birds in the world. Some eagles weigh as

much as twelve or thirteen pounds and have a wingspan of about seven feet.

The nests of eagles are called eyries (AIR eez). They are built mainly of sticks, and are often lined with fresh green leaves while they are being used. Once a year, the female lays one or two eggs, and they are carefully tended, sometimes even by the male eagle, until they hatch in about forty days. Both parents then guard the nest and take food to the young.

At about eleven or twelve weeks, a curious thing happens. If the eaglets have not yet ventured forth on their own, the parent eagle "stirs" or rocks the nest, tipping the eaglets out! The young eaglets flap about in panic, still novices at this flying business. The parent eagle hovers watchfully, waiting for the critical moment. With wings spread wide, the eagle then swoops down underneath those babies and delivers them back to the security of the eyrie.

Ours is a God of powerful gentleness. Ours is a God whose timing is perfect. Like the parent eagle, he is sensitive to our needs. He knows when the nest has become too comfortable and needs a little stirring. He, too, watches carefully, and, as with spread wings, catches us up, bringing us to himself. But he wants us to learn from our fluttering and flapping. He wants us to leave behind our panic and to learn to wait on him. Then, with our eyes on our parent eagle, we will begin to know what it means to soar on eagle's wings!

Today we praise you, O God, for eagle's wings that keep us safe, that help us soar, and that bring us to yourself.

# 22

## Author and Editor
**Scripture:** Ephesians 1:3–10; 2:10

Let us fix our eyes on Jesus, the *author and
[editor\*]* of our faith. [Heb. 12:2]

There isn't a human author who doesn't, or
wouldn't, benefit from a good editor. The author con-
ceives and births the idea, but a second pair of eyes
sees it in a different way and with a fresh perspective.

A case can also be made for the idea that human
editors—those who perfect, polish, and put on the
finishing touches, those who see the work through
to completion—need authors.

As our Author, Jesus Christ conceived the very
idea of us before the foundation of the world. He
made possible both our birth and our new birth.

But he hasn't stopped there. He has the will, the
ability, and the authority to see us—his workman-

---

\*The Greek has been translated "finisher" (KJV) and "perfecter" (RSV,
NIV, and Ryrie). My rendering, "editor," has much the same connotation.

ship, his poem (Eph. 2:10)—through to completion. Paul tells the Philippians that he is confident that "he who began a good work in you will carry it on to completion until the day of Christ Jesus" (Phil. 1:6).

Sometimes we question or chafe at all the editing that is prescribed for us. But ours is not an Editor capable of error or capriciousness. Unlikely as it may seem at times, we will someday be all that he means for us to be, his masterpiece.

Worship Jesus Christ, both Author and Editor, with me today!

# 23

## The Great Shepherd

**Scripture:** Psalm 23; Matthew 18:12–14;
John 10:1–18; Hebrews 13:20–21

. . . our Lord Jesus, that *great Shepherd* of the
sheep . . . [Heb. 13:20]

"I am the good shepherd; I know my sheep and
my sheep know me—just as the Father knows
me and I know the Father—and I lay down my
life for the sheep." [John 10:14]

A good shepherd, or pastor, must have a
combination of almost paradoxical qualities.

We who are not shepherds tend to think of a pastoral scene as being peaceful and quiet. The picture
is full of lush greens, blue sky, and a crystal-clear
pool of water. No sounds more harsh than those of
chirping birds can be heard. Our image of the shepherd tends to be that of a person both gentle and
patient. The good shepherd thoughtfully provides the
best nourishment and care possible for his sheep. He

is willing to risk personal hardship and danger for them . . . With the picture as sketched so far, we like thinking of ourselves as sheep, under such a shepherd!

But sheep are stupid creatures. Often they don't have the sense to follow the shepherd, and he must nudge or even push them from behind or alongside. Sheep are willful creatures, often straying, searching for something better, somewhere else.

The good shepherd knows each one of his sheep by name, and each is important to him. He will leave the rest of the flock to search for one that wanders off. The good shepherd persistently combs the countryside until he locates the missing sheep.

Here the pastoral picture changes. The once blue sky darkens with an approaching storm. The sheep is caught in a thorn bush at the brink of a precipice. The good shepherd has to act swiftly, forcefully. He places his shepherd's crook firmly around the neck of his sheep. Holding aside some of the thorny branches with one arm, the shepherd pulls—yes, yanks—his sheep free from the bush, bringing some of the thorns and smaller branches with it.

Having found shelter, the good shepherd has to pull out the thorns, one by one, as his sheep bleats in pain.

On the way home, the shepherd has to kill a wild animal which would otherwise have attacked. The sheep trembles and is afraid.

The good shepherd is indeed gentle and patient, a loving provider of care and nourishment. He is also strong and able, and will push or pull hard when love for his sheep dictates that he do so.

The God of love my Shepherd is,
And He that doth me feed:
While He is mine and I am His,
What can I want or need?

He leads me to the tender grass
Where I both feed and rest;
Then to the streams that gently pass,
In both I have the best.

Or if I stray, He doth convert,
And bring my mind in frame:
And all this not for my desert,
But for His holy name.

Yea, in death's shady, black abode
Well may I walk, not fear,
For Thou art with me, and Thy rod
To guide, Thy staff to bear.

Surely Thy sweet and wondrous love
Shall measure all my days;
And as it never shall remove,
So neither shall my praise. Amen.

—George Herbert
(based on Psalm 23)

# 24

## Lamb

**Scripture:** John 1:29–34; Revelation 5:12; 1 Corinthians 5:7–8

Abraham answered, "God himself will provide the lamb for the burnt offering, my son." [Gen. 22:8]

"Tell the whole community of Israel that on the tenth day of this month each man is to take a lamb for his family, one for each household." [Exod. 12:3]

He was led like a lamb to the slaughter,
    and as a sheep before her shearers is silent,
    so he did not open his mouth. [Isa. 53:7b]

The next day John saw Jesus coming toward him and said, "Look, the *Lamb* of God, who takes away the sin of the world." [John 1:29]

[You were redeemed] with the precious blood of Christ, a lamb without blemish or defect. [1 Peter 1:19]

Then I saw a Lamb, looking as if it had been slain, standing in the center of the throne. . . . In a loud voice they sang:

"Worthy is the Lamb, who was slain,
   to receive power and wealth and wisdom and
      strength
and honor and glory and praise!" [Rev. 5:6, 12]

". . . they have washed their robes and made them white in the blood of the Lamb. . . . For the Lamb at the center of the throne will be their shepherd." [Rev. 7:14b, 17a]

Can it be that the Creator of all the galaxies was also named the Lamb? The gentle creature of whom the poet asked:

Little lamb, who made thee?
   Dost thou know who made thee?
Gave thee life, and bid thee feed
By the stream and o'er the mead;
Gave thee clothing of delight,
Softest clothing, woolly, bright;
Gave thee such a tender voice,
Making all the vales rejoice?
   Little lamb, who made thee?
   Dost thou know who made thee?
   Little lamb, I'll tell thee,
   Little lamb, I'll tell thee.
He is callèd by thy name,
For He calls Himself a Lamb.
He is meek, and He is mild,
He became a little child.
I a child, and thou a lamb,
We are callèd by His name.

80

Little lamb, God bless thee!
Little lamb, God bless thee!

—William Blake, *Songs of Innocence*

The lamb, even today, symbolizes innocence and purity. Only a pure white lamb could be a sacrifice. A spotted lamb was not acceptable. The sacrificial lamb could not have any blemish or deformity. It could not harbor a parasite or suffer from any ailment. It had to be the first-born of its mother.

The offering of a lamb had to be from an obedient heart in order to be acceptable. This was true of the very first offering mentioned in Scripture, Abel's offering of a lamb from his flock (Gen. 4), and continues to be true for every offering thereafter. King Saul's proposed offering was rejected because he had been disobedient (1 Sam. 15). He was told, "To obey is better than sacrifice, and to heed is better than the fat of rams" (15:22). The offering of the Lamb was an offering of obedience. The writer of Hebrews says of Christ, the Lamb, "Although he was a son, he learned obedience from what he suffered" (Heb. 5:8).

For the offering to be complete, the blood of the Lamb had to be shed. "And without the shedding of blood there is no forgiveness" (Heb. 9:22).

All the animals sacrificed in the time of the Old Testament were object lessons, pointing toward the one sufficient, worthy sacrifice. Because all mankind has sinned, the only one who could provide an acceptable sacrifice was God himself. Abraham was more right than he knew when he told Isaac, "God himself will provide the lamb for the burnt offering . . ." (Gen. 22:8).

God's Lamb, holy, pure, perfect, and altogether

worthy, shed his blood as an offering to atone for our sins. For us, the Creator of the galaxies became a Child, who became the Lamb of God.

The wonder is that "we are callèd by His name"!

What does it mean for me, today, that I am called a lamb?

What does it mean for me, today, that Jesus is the Lamb?

"Worthy is the Lamb, who was slain,
To receive power and wealth and wisdom and strength
And honor and glory and praise!" [Rev. 5:12]

# 25

## Immanuel — God with Us

**Scripture:** Matthew 1:18–25

"The virgin will be with child and will give birth to a son, and they will call him *Immanuel*"— which means, "God with us." [Matt. 1:23]

*I*mmanuel *means a restored relationship.* When sin entered the world there was a real sense in which the holy God was prevented from being with the men and women he had created. The God-man had to come in order to bring about a reconciliation. It is because of the death and resurrection of the Immanuel that we can know that God is with us.

*Immanuel means there is One who knows how we feel, who identifies with us.* Sometimes God gives us a hint of his kind of empathy through another person. A young mother had ventured out to the grocery store with her three small children. It was her first such trip after the birth of her third baby. As she approached the check-out lanes, the three-year-old managed to knock a large jar of grape jelly onto the floor, leaving in her wake a huge puddle of broken glass and gooey grape jelly. The five-year-old announced in no uncertain terms that she *had* to go to the bathroom, *now*. The baby's wails announced loudly to the entire store that he was hungry. Every check-out lane had a long line of shoppers with heavily laden carts. A woman at the head of one of the lanes steered the young mother in front of her.

"You go first," she said. "I have five children of my own, and I know how you feel."

*Immanuel means we don't have to feel alone.* There is an aloneness that comes even in the midst of a large crowd of people—just ask any young child who has ever been lost in such a crowd. There is the aloneness of being misunderstood. There is the aloneness of being in an empty house or apartment, all by oneself, night after night. And there is the aloneness of trying to carry a heavy load without help.

Immanuel! God is with us! Appropriate the significance of that fact with me today.

# 26

## Potter
**Scripture:** Isaiah 64:8; Jeremiah 18:6;
Romans 9:21; Ephesians 2:10;
2 Corinthians 4:7

. . . you are the *potter*;
we are all the work of your hand. [Isa. 64:8b]

"O house of Israel, can I not do with you as this
potter does?" declares the LORD. "Like clay in
the hand of the potter, so are you in my hand.
. . ." [Jer. 18:6]

Ouch! I don't like the way You're pressing
and squeezing me! . . .

That's to work the air bubbles out, You say? So I
won't crack later on? Oh . . .

You wouldn't *throw* me on that moving wheel,
would You? It's spinning so fast, I'm not ready for
anything like that yet . . .

But You're ready? And that's all that matters?
Hmmm . . .

Hey! This hurts! Don't You think about *my* feelings at all? . . .

Check out the scars in the Potter's hands . . . What kind of an answer is that anyway? . . .

I don't think I like being this shape. And while we're on that subject, the color of the glaze You've chosen for me isn't at all becoming, if You ask me . . .

You didn't ask me? Oh . . .

Surely You aren't going to make me just another ordinary water pot, are You? I had so hoped to be something unique—a priceless object d'art . . .

Wait a minute! You weren't planning to put me in the kiln, were You? It's hot in there! Why, if I do get out of that oven, I won't ever be the same again! . . .

That was Your plan, You say? To make me strong and usable? A jar to hold living Water? That the excellency of the power may be of God, and not of . . . oh. I think I'm beginning to see.

"But who are you, O man, to talk back to God? 'Shall what is formed say to him who formed it, "Why did you make me like this?" ' Does not the potter have the right to make out of the same lump of clay some pottery for noble purposes and some for common use?" (Rom. 9:20–21).

Have thine own way, Lord! Have thine own way!
Thou art the Potter; I am the clay.
Mold me and make me, after thy will,
While I am waiting, yielded and still.

—Adelaide A. Pollard, 1902

# 27

## Abba, Father
**Scripture:** Luke 15:11–31

... you received the Spirit of sonship. And by
him we cry, "*Abba*, Father." The Spirit himself
testifies with our spirit that we are God's
children. Now if we are children, then we are
heirs—heirs of God and co-heirs with Christ. ...
[Rom. 8:15b–17a]

"This, then, is how you should pray:
'Our Father in heaven,
hallowed be your name. ...' " [Matt. 6:9]

"When Israel was a child, I loved him,
    and out of Egypt I called my son.
It was I who taught Ephraim to walk,
    taking them by the arms. ..." [Hos. 11:1, 3a]

Be imitators of God, therefore, as dearly loved
children. ... [Eph. 5:1]

*F*atherhood is initiated by the act of the father, not the child. No child can choose his own fa-

ther. In the same way, our relationship with our heavenly Father exists because he took the initiative.

*Fathers often have children who resemble them.* That is how it should be with our heavenly Father. In a human relationship, a child may look like his father because he shares some of the same genes and chromosomes. Our heavenly Father has created us in his own image. So we resemble him in a way his other creatures do not. In addition, little children watch their fathers and become like them by imitating them. Children learn to copy mannerisms, speech patterns, and other habits. They may try on a parent's shoes or clothing in order to be like the parent. They learn to value what the parent values. In much the same way, we who are God's children are to imitate him and to work at becoming children who resemble their Father.

*A father is accessible to his child.* A busy and important business executive has an outer office where secretaries screen his calls and where visitors wait. They may enter the inner office only after they are properly announced. But when the executive's young son arrives on the scene, the formalities are dispensed with. The child calls excitedly, "Daddy," toddles in, and plops himself on his father's lap. Our heavenly Father has made himself accessible to us. We need not wait to be announced or to have our credentials checked. He is always ready to hear us and to converse with us.

*A father's child is usually his heir.* The heir is the one who is legally entitled to receive what has belonged to the father. Think of all that belongs to our heavenly Father! Because of our relationship with him, we are legally entitled to receive it! As the apostle

Paul put it, "Now if we are children, then we are heirs—heirs of God, and co-heirs with Christ" (Rom. 8:17a).

*The father loves his child.* There are human fathers who don't love their children. Sometimes God puts in our path the child of such a person, and we have the opportunity to love that child with a fatherlike love. Without a human example, such a child has a hard time seeing God as his Father. Some of us have been blessed with human fathers who do love us dearly. We have been given an object lesson, a hint of what being loved by the heavenly Father is like! Our loving Father longs to teach us how to walk.

> It was I who taught Ephraim to walk,
>     taking them by the arms,

writes the prophet Hosea of the Father God (11:3a). The love of our heavenly Father is not based on what we can do for him. It is not conditioned on our perfect obedience. It is a love that allows us to make our own mistakes, that we may grow from them. It is a love that will discipline us, so we will become the people we were created to be. The Father's love is something we cannot seek, earn, buy, or deserve. It is a love that desires the very best for us, and knows what that best is. "Every good and perfect gift is from above, coming down from the Father of the heavenly lights, who does not change like shifting shadows" (James 1:17).

> Fatherlike, he tends and spares us;
> Well our feeble frame he knows;
> In his hands he gently bears us,

Rescues us from all our foes;
Praise him, praise him,
Praise him, praise him,
Widely as his mercy goes.

—Henry F. Lyte, 1834
(based on Psalm 103)

Our Father in heaven, hallowed be your name!

# 28

## Creator
**Scripture:** Psalm 8; Isaiah 40:25–26, 28

"To whom will you compare me?
  Or who is my equal?" says the Holy One.
Lift your eyes and look to the heavens:
  Who created all these?
He who brings out the starry host one by one,
  and calls them each by name.
Because of his great power and mighty strength,
  not one of them is missing.

Do you not know?
  Have you not heard?
The LORD is the everlasting God,
  the *Creator* of the ends of the earth. [Isa.
    40:25–26, 28a]

We like to think we are creative, and indeed we are prolific makers of things. In the twentieth century alone, man has invented the automobile, the computer, vehicles which have carried him to the moon and back, radio, television—the list could fill a small book.

To create is "to cause to exist, to bring into being." Only God himself can truly cause something to exist. Only God himself can take meaningless nothing, without form and void, and make of it something significant.

It is because we have indeed been created in God's image that we have the capacity to take what we have been given and form from it something fresh.

The conception and subsequent birth of a child is a glorious, creative act—God allows us to participate in it. But who really caused that child to exist? Who really brought him into being?

Using the gifts God has put at our disposal, we as God's image-bearers paint, we compose or perform music, we sculpt, we write, we weave, we knit, we cook, we sew, and sometimes we come up with something that has a fresh sound or a fresh look to it. Our work went into this "creation," and people sometimes laud our efforts as creative or imaginative. But the best creations of the image-bearers are at most reminders of, and reflections of, our Creator.

Creator God, forgive us for clinging so foolishly to that which we consider "our" creation. Help us to lay these creations and the recognition or lack of recognition they bring us at the feet of the only One truly worthy of the name *Creator*.

> The spacious firmament on high,
> With all the blue ethereal sky,
> And spangled heav'ns, a shining frame,
> Their great Original proclaim.
> Th' unwearied sun, from day to day,

Does his Creator's pow'r display,
And publishes to ev'ry land
The work of an almighty hand.

Soon as the evening shades prevail,
The moon takes up the wondrous tale,
And nightly to the list'ning earth
Repeats the story of her birth;
Whilst all the stars that round her burn,
And all the planets in their turn,
Confirm the tidings as they roll,
And spread the truth from pole to pole.

What though, in solemn silence, all
Move round this dark terrestrial ball?
What though nor real voice nor sound
Amidst their radiant orbs be found?
In reason's ear they all rejoice,
And utter forth a glorious voice;
For ever singing as they shine,
"The hand that made us is divine."

—Joseph Addison, 1712
(based on Psalm 19)

# 29

## Owner of the Cattle on a Thousand Hills

**Scripture:** Psalm 50:7–11

"I am God, your God. . . .
For every animal of the forest is mine,
    and *the cattle on a thousand hills.*
I know every bird in the mountains,
    and the creatures of the field are mine. . . .
    For the world is mine, and all that is in it."
        [Ps. 50:7b, 10–11, 12b]

And my God will meet all your needs according
to his glorious riches in Christ Jesus. [Phil. 4:19]

"So do not worry, saying, 'What shall we eat?' or
'What shall we drink?' or 'What shall we wear?'
For the pagans run after all these things, and
your heavenly Father knows that you need them.
But seek first his kingdom and his righteousness,
and all these things will be given you as well."
[Matt. 6:31–33]

To four-year-old Justin, the birthday gift from his grandparents was only a small blue piece of paper with some words and numbers on it. With only his four years of experience, he failed to understand that on that small blue piece of paper was a promise that, at his request, a certain bank would make fifty dollars available to him. Justin failed to understand the generous gift that had been made available to him.

How many of us are like Justin! We fail both to appreciate and to appropriate all that our God has put at our disposal! All the power of heaven and earth, peace that defies human understanding, the wherewithal to meet all our needs—these are in the bank for us, and we have a blank check to draw on this account.

What does it mean to be a recipient of God's providence? What are the "incomparable riches of [God's] grace, expressed in his kindness to us in Christ Jesus" (Eph. 2:7)? Like Justin, because we don't always see something tangible in front of us, we underestimate what we have been given. Maybe we need to take the advice of the old hymn and "count [our] many blessings, name them, one by one, And it will surprise [us] what the Lord has done."

A story is told of an old Indian whose need to take stock of what he had at his disposal was well understood by the local banker. From time to time, the Indian would enter the bank and say, "Grass all gone, sheep all sick, waterholes all dry." The banker would nod, lead the Indian back to the room which held the safety deposit boxes, and unlock a certain drawer. The Indian would spend some time counting and examining the bags of silver in his deposit box, and then he would say to the banker, "Plenty of grass, sheep well, waterholes full." The external circumstances hadn't changed, but after he took stock of his resources, his perspective changed.

Praise to the Lord, who o'er all things so wondrously
    reigneth,
Shelters thee under his wings, yea, so gently
    sustaineth!
Hast thou not seen how thy desires e'er have been
Granted in what he ordaineth?

—Joachim Neander, 1680

# 30

## Lion of the Tribe of Judah

**Scripture:** Job 10:16; Jeremiah 49:19;
Ezekiel 19:1–4; Hosea 5:14–15;
11:9–10; 13:4–8; Amos 3:4; Revelation
5:5

"Like a lion coming up from Jordan's thickets
   to a rich pastureland,
I [the Lord] will chase Edom from its land in an
   instant. . . .
Who is like me and who can challenge me?
   And what shepherd can stand against me?"
   [Jer. 49:19]

Then one of the elders said to me, "Do not weep!
See, *the Lion of the tribe of Judah* . . . has
triumphed. He is able to open the scroll and its
seven seals." [Rev. 5:5]

The King of Beasts! Majestic, powerful,
beautiful, awful. We shudder at his roar. We shiver to
think of the potential of those claws and teeth. He

must never be considered tame. We are the Lion's adopted cubs.

The One named Lion of the tribe of Judah is the same one the prophet Ezekiel writes about:

> " 'What a lioness was your mother
>     among the lions!
> She lay down among the young lions
>     and reared her cubs.' " [19:2]

She nursed them, chased off intruders, and taught them all the ways of a lion.

> " 'She brought up one of her cubs,
>     and he became a strong lion.
> He learned to tear the prey
>     and he devoured men.
> The nations heard about him,
>     and he was trapped in their pit.
> They led him with hooks
>     to the land of Egypt.' " [19:3–4]

We are the Lion's adopted cubs—we have been fed, protected, and taught.

Unchallengeable, the Lion chases away his enemies in an instant. No mere shepherd dares stand against him (Jer. 49:19). And we are the Lion's cubs!

The Lion cubs forget who feeds them, and become proud. Since cubs are the privileged progeny of the Lion, they are the ones he loves enough to punish. The Lion destroys his enemies, but punishes his cubs so that "in their misery they will earnestly seek [him]" (Hos. 5:15). We are the Lion's adopted cubs.

Sometimes a cub holds his head high—thinking

for a moment that he is the King instead of the cub. At such a time, the Lion stalks his own cub and again displays his awesome power (Job 10:16).

C. S. Lewis, in his chronicles of Narnia, paints a wonderful picture of Aslan, the Great Lion:

'Ooh!' said Susan, 'I'd thought he was a man. Is he—quite safe? I shall feel rather nervous about meeting a lion.'

'That you will, dearie, and no mistake,' said Mrs. Beaver. 'If there's anyone who can appear before Aslan without their knees knocking, they're either braver than most, or just silly.'

'Then he isn't safe?' said Lucy.

'Safe?' said Mr. Beaver. 'Don't you hear what Mrs. Beaver tells you? Who said anything about safe? 'Course he isn't safe. But he's good. He's the King, I tell you.'*

Good and terrible Lion,

"You are worthy . . .
    to receive glory and honor and power,
for you created all things,
    and by your will they were created
    and have their being." [Rev. 4:11]

*C. S. Lewis, *The Lion, the Witch, and the Wardrobe* (London: Collins, 1950), chap. 8, p. 77.

# 31

## A Consuming Fire
**Scripture:** Malachi 3:1–4

... our "God is a *consuming fire*." [Heb. 12:29]

"Then suddenly the Lord you are seeking will come to his temple. ..." But who can endure the day of his coming? Who can stand when he appears? For he will be like a refiner's fire. ... He will sit as a refiner and purifier of silver; he will purify the Levites and refine them like gold and silver. Then the LORD will have men who will bring offerings in righteousness. ... [Mal. 3:1–3]

By day the LORD went ahead of them in a pillar of cloud to guide them on their way and by night in a pillar of fire to give them light, so they could travel by day or night. Neither the pillar of cloud by day nor the pillar of fire by night left its place in front of the people. [Exod. 13:21–22]

The neon lights of our city streets pale in

comparison. No invention of man could have lit up the sky like God's towering inferno!

The pillar of fire, although it was probably regarded with reverence, did not strike terror in the hearts of the Israelites who saw it. A mother, putting her little one to bed, could assure him that he need not fear. The fiery night light at the entrance of the camp meant that God himself was with them, watching as they slept. If ever the desert night grew chill, God's fire was their warmth. Sometimes night travel was a welcome relief from travel during the desert's day-time heat. The fiery pillar would lead the way, showing the Israelites where they were to go. No one needed a flashlight! The pillar of fire provided light and direction. Every night God's fire would be there with them. His people could count on it. The pillar of fire was their comfort.

The God who is a comforting fire is also a consuming fire. The fire of God fell from heaven and utterly devoured the water-drenched sacrifice of God's prophet Elijah (1 Kings 18:38).

Our God is like a refiner's fire. Only a very small percentage of each chunk of ore is pure gold. The ore is full of impurities. To extract the gold so that it can be used, the ore must be placed in a furnace and sub-jected to tremendous temperatures. At last, the once solid ore melts, and the gold can be separated.

There is a comforting aspect to this consuming Fire. It is not the sons of Jacob the Cheat who are consumed (Mal. 3:6)—it is their impurity and sin. Being melted and having all but the gold stripped away, then being melted again and shaped—it is a painful process. But the Refiner knows what he is about.

When through fiery trials thy pathway shall lie,
My grace, all sufficient, shall be thy supply.
The flame shall not hurt thee; I only design
Thy dross to consume, and thy gold to refine.

—"K" in Rippon's *Selection*, 1787

What can be our response? The writer of Hebrews
suggests, ". . . let us be thankful, and so worship God
acceptably with reverence and awe, for our 'God is a
consuming fire' " (Heb. 12:28b–29).

# 32

## Man of Sorrows
**Scripture:** Isaiah 53

He was despised and rejected by men,
  a *man of sorrows*, and familiar with suffering.
Like one from whom men hide their faces
  he was despised, and we esteemed him not.
  [Isa. 53:3]

B eing booked! The process is completely depersonalizing. One's wallet, watch, and other possessions are confiscated. Often one's own clothing must be exchanged for institutional garb. Fingerprinting is required. Even one's own name must be exchanged for an identifying number. This impersonal number must be held high while the police photographer takes "mug shots." The details are placed in the official police record. The one who is "booked" is now numbered with the transgressors.

The Man of Sorrows was "numbered with the transgressors" (Isa. 53:12). In the divine record, he

103

was booked for all the sins of all mankind. Well he understands the stigma and the humiliation attached:

> He was despised and rejected by men,
>   a man of sorrows, and familiar with suffering.
> Like one from whom men hide their faces. . . .

Worse still, the Man of Sorrows knows the indescribable horror of having God hide his face: "My God, my God, why have you forsaken me?" he cried (Matt. 27:46).

Playwright Thornton Wilder spoke more truth than perhaps he realized when in *Our Town* he wrote: "In love's service, only the wounded can serve." The Man of Sorrows came to be pierced, crushed, and wounded (Isa. 53:5–6). And he came because he loved us.

The suffering, the sorrow, and the wounds we sometimes experience pale in contrast to those of the Man of Sorrows. It hardly seems appropriate to use the same words to describe them. But the Man of Sorrows doesn't turn from us. He knows what we feel. He, of all who ever walked this earth, knows how to empathize with us. He became sin for us, and in so doing, our tears became his tears, our grief, his grief, and our pain, his pain. And "by his wounds we are healed." He took the permanence out of pain.

> Man of Sorrows! What a name
> For the Son of God, who came
> Ruined sinners to reclaim:
> Hallelujah! What a Savior!
>
> Bearing shame and scoffing rude,
> In my place condemned he stood,
> Sealed my pardon with his blood:
> Hallelujah! What a Savior!

Guilty, vile, and helpless, we;
Spotless Lamb of God was he;
Full atonement! Can it be?
Hallelujah! What a Savior!

Lifted up was he to die,
"It is finished!" was his cry:
Now in heaven exalted high:
Hallelujah! What a Savior!

When he comes, our glorious King,
All his ransomed home to bring;
Then anew this song we'll sing:
Hallelujah! What a Savior!

—Philip P. Bliss (1838–1876)

Man of Sorrows, we kneel before you this day and
exclaim, "What a Savior!"

# 33

## El Shaddai

**Scripture:** Genesis 43:14; Psalm 131:2–3

When Abram was ninety-nine years old, the
LORD appeared to him and said, "I am God
Almighty (*El Shaddai*)". . . . "I have made you a
father of many nations. I will make you very
fruitful; I will make nations of you, and kings
will come from you." [Gen. 17:1a, 5b–6]

"And may God Almighty (El Shaddai) grant you
mercy before the man so that he will let your
other brother and Benjamin come back with you.
. . ." [Gen. 43:14]

". . . because of your father's God (the El), who
     helps you,
   because of the Almighty (Shaddai) who blesses
     you
   with blessings of the heavens above,
   blessings of the deep that lies below,
   blessings of the breast and womb." [Gen.
     49:25]

But Zion said, "The LORD has forsaken me,
   the LORD has forgotten me."

"Can a mother forget the baby at her breast
　and have no compassion on the child she has
　　borne?
Though she may forget,
　I will not forget you!
See, I have engraved you on the palms of my
　hands. . . ." [Isa. 49:14−16a]

But I have stilled and quieted my soul;
　like a weaned child with its mother,
　like a weaned child is my soul within me.
O Israel, put your hope in the LORD. . . . [Ps.
　131:2−3]

"O Jerusalem, Jerusalem, you who kill the
prophets and stone those sent to you, how often I
have longed to gather your children together, as a
hen gathers her chicks under her wings, but you
were not willing." [Matt. 23:37]

I n somewhat the same way as God is bigger
than any and all of the names we can name him, he
is also bigger than the images our minds conjure of
a single gender. Scripture, in showing us facets of
who God is, sometimes portrays him in terms we
associate with the feminine gender.

The Hebrew name *El Shaddai* comes as close to
capturing this aspect of God as does any of his names.
The traditional translations of Scripture have consis-
tently rendered this name "Almighty." But to appreciate its full flavor, it will be helpful to examine its
Hebrew roots.* *El* is a shortened form of *Elohim*. It
sets forth the might, the strength, and the excellence
of God. *Shad* is the Hebrew word for breast. *Shaddai*

*Robert B. Girdlestone, *Synonyms of the Old Testament* (reprint ed.,
Grand Rapids: Eerdmans, 1974), pp. 32−34.

pictures God's fullness or bounty, his tenderness, his generosity, his desire to nurture us and make us fruitful. In one name, God's attributes of might and tenderness are brought together!

When Abram was ninety-nine years old, El Shaddai appeared to him and said, "I have made you a father. . . ." Speaking in strictly human terms, it takes a woman to go to a man and say, "I'm going to make you a father!" Sometimes this announcement comes as a shock. Often the shocking aspect of this news is mingled with a great deal of joy and thanksgiving, along with some apprehension. Certainly all of these emotions were present as El Shaddai's announcement was received. "You will be very fruitful—nations and kings will come from you" (paraphrase, Gen. 17:6).

It was God himself who gave birth to the nation of Israel. The prophet Isaiah described the birthing process thus: "like a woman in childbirth I cry out, I gasp and pant" (42:14).

Jacob is full of anxiety as he is about to send his beloved son Benjamin off to Egypt in response to the whimsical demand of the ruler who dispensed food. "May [El Shaddai] grant you mercy before the man . . . ," he cries (Gen. 43:14).

Later, as Jacob is pronouncing God's blessing on his son Joseph, he says, "Because of the El and the Shaddai, may you have blessings of the breast and the womb" (paraphrase, Gen. 49:25).

Isaiah, in describing the love of God, says it is greater than that of a nursing mother. A unique bonding occurs as the mother holds her child close to her breast. She is the source of all the infant needs for nourishment as she holds him close to the warmth of her body, within the sound of her heartbeat and secure in the safety of her arms.

A further dimension to this picture is added by the psalmist in Psalm 131. The psalmist feels like a weaned child. *"Why* am I being deprived of what, from my point of view, seems so good and so right?" he may have been asking himself. "This is what I need, God. Why can't I have it?"

Have you ever asked God these sorts of questions?

God, who, like a mother, knows that the growing child must move beyond breast milk, still holds the child close enough to hear the divine heartbeat, allowing the child the warmth and security of being held tightly in divine arms.

The child's questions may still be unanswered. But his soul is stilled and quieted, "like a weaned child with its mother" (Ps. 131:2), because he knows, without any doubt, Who is holding him!

El Shaddai, almighty, tender God. Hold us close to your heart today.

# 34

## Advocate
**Scripture:** Hebrews 2:16; 4:15–16

My little children, I am writing this to you so that you may not sin; but if any one does sin, we have an *advocate* with the Father, Jesus Christ the righeous. . . . [1 John 2:1, RSV]

**W**hat if you had to stand before the great eternal Judge and present your own case? Imagine yourself, standing alone at the bar, clothed in your own very best efforts. The prosecutor is a shrewd one. He has all the resources of hell itself to draw on. The key exhibit in this case is your own obedience to the law of God. What would the verdict be?

Scripture leaves no room for question. All have sinned and come short of the glory of God, writes the apostle Paul (Rom. 3:23). Clearly, the verdict would have to be guilty.

But we don't have to present our own case. We have an advocate, one who stands in our place to speak on our behalf. Our Advocate has the necessary qualifications. He is familiar with our case, and has been since before the earth was founded (Isa. 40:21–28).

Our Advocate prepares his clients. He knows that, dressed in our own righteousness, we don't stand a chance. At great personal cost, he has seen to it that appropriate clothing has been provided us.

A certain defendant awaited the day of his trial in jail. He was scheduled to appear before a judge who was known for his fastidious attention to proper courtroom dress and decorum. Male defendants who appeared before him were expected to wear a coat and tie. But this defendant did not own coat or tie, and had no means of procuring them. Before the appointed hour of the trial, the defendant received the appropriate clothing, specially delivered to him. The clothing had been sent by the judge himself, from his personal wardrobe.

When we stand before God, we will be able to stand there in clothing provided from the Judge's own wardrobe. We will be able to wear the righteousness of God himself!

When we stand before God, we will not need to stand alone. Our Advocate, Jesus Christ the Righteous, will be standing with us. He will plead our case, and already we can rejoice in the verdict.

My advocate appears for my defense on high;
The Father bows his ears and lays his thunder by.
Not all that hell or sin can say
Shall turn his heart, his love away.

—Isaac Watts, 1709

# 35

## Bridegroom
**Scripture:** Isaiah 62:5b

... as a bridegroom rejoices over his bride,
so will your God rejoice over you. [Isa. 62:5b]

"The bride belongs to the *bridegroom.* The friend
who attends the bridegroom waits and listens for
him, and is full of joy when he hears the
bridegroom's voice. That joy is mine, and it is
now complete." [John 3:29]

In our twentieth-century society, a wedding
typically tends to focus on the bride. The bride's family hosts it, issues the invitations, and plans and pays for the reception. When the wedding march begins, all eyes look in the direction of the approaching bride. Few even notice, until after the fact, that the groom has also entered to the accompaniment of the same music!

But a marriage ceremony was very different in

Middle Eastern cultures during the time when the Scriptures were being written.

The bridegroom and his family hosted the wedding. This is clear from the account of the wedding at Cana, where Jesus did his first miracle (John 2:9—the bridegroom supplied the wine). It is also indicated in a parable Jesus told (Matt. 22:2). A king prepared a wedding banquet for his son. The wedding invitations were personally delivered by servants from the bridegroom's household.

The bridegroom is the key figure in the wedding procession (Matt. 25:1–10). All the attendants are to be in readiness for the bridegroom's arrival. The psalmist compares the sun to "a bridegroom coming forth from his pavilion" (Ps. 19:5). The bridegroom's arrival is a glorious moment, and from that point on, the excitement crescendoes.

The bridegroom has gone to great personal expense and effort in order that this wedding could take place. In preparation, "a bridegroom adorns his head like a priest" (Isa. 61:10). A priest's head was anointed with oil as a symbol that he was set apart for the special purpose of offering sacrifices to God on behalf of the people. Our bridegroom, Jesus Christ, is worthy of the adornment of a priest. He has offered the supreme sacrifice—himself—on behalf of his bride.

Our bridegroom has even provided clothing for the bride to wear: "fine linen, bright and clean" (Rev. 19:8).

> The bride eyes not her garment, but her dear bridegroom's face;
> [She] will not gaze at glory, but on [her] King of grace;

113

Not at the crown He gifteth, but on His pierced hand:
The Lamb is all the glory of Emmanuel's land.

—Anne R. Cousin, 1857, based upon
Samuel Rutherford (1600–1661)

The wedding supper will certainly be the wedding feast to end all wedding feasts. The angel who described the plans for the celebration to the apostle John said that those who were invited were blessed (Rev. 19:9).

There will be a great multitude at this wedding, all at the invitation of the Father of the Bridegroom, God himself! They will greet the arrival of the Bridegroom with shouting that sounds like the roar of rushing waters and peals of loud thunder.

"Hallelujah!
  For our Lord God Almighty reigns.
Let us rejoice and be glad
  and give him glory!
For the wedding of the Lamb has come,
  And his bride has made herself ready." [Rev.
  19:6b–7]

O Jesus Christ, our Bridegroom! Help us to prepare for your coming with the meticulous care of a bride-to-be. Help us to anticipate your coming with the enthusiasm of a bride-to-be. "Amen. Come, Lord Jesus" (Rev. 22:20b).

# 36

## Prince of Peace
**Scripture:** Ephesians 2:11–18

And he will be called . . . *Prince of Peace.* [Isa. 9:6b]

And the peace of God, which transcends all understanding, will guard your hearts and your minds in Christ Jesus. [Phil. 4:7]

"Peace I leave with you; my peace I give you. I do not give to you as the world gives. Do not let your hearts be troubled and do not be afraid." [John 14:27]

"I have told you these things, so that in me you may have peace. In this world you will have trouble. But take heart! I have overcome the world." [John 16:33]

But the fruit of the Spirit is . . . peace. . . . [Gal. 5:22]

S ee if you can paint in your mind a picture

of peace. Most of us will visualize a quiet, tranquil, well-ordered scene with an absence of any sort of conflict. But when we look at the picture of the Prince of Peace presented in Scripture, it shatters our mental images.

It is noteworthy that the very first promise of the One who would come and who would be called Prince of Peace states that "he will crush [Satan's] head" (Gen. 3:15). The apostle Paul picks up on this image in Romans 16:20: "The God of peace will soon crush Satan under your feet. The grace of our Lord Jesus be with you." Crushing someone under foot is hardly a tranquil activity. The act of crushing seems more warlike than peaceful. Paul describes the believer by using the metaphor of a soldier putting on his armor in preparation for battle. The soldier's footwear is to be the "readiness that comes from the gospel of peace" (Eph. 6:15).

Perhaps one reason for the apparent contradiction is that we have lost some of the original Hebrew meaning for the word. The root of the Hebrew *shalom* or *shalam* (peace) may originally have signified oneness, completeness, or perfection.*

If peace involves perfection, is there hope for any of us? Listen to the words of Jesus, "Peace I leave with you. My peace I give you." Christ Jesus offers us the perfection of his heart! God sees Christ's perfection and considers us perfect in him. Like a strong magnet pulls scattered bits of iron into line with itself, so his strong and perfect heart pulls our hearts into conformity with his.

*Robert B. Girdlestone, *Synonyms of the Old Testament* (reprint ed., Grand Rapids: Eerdmans, 1974), pp. 95–98.

In order to restore our oneness with God, in order to perfect us and make us complete, the greatest act of violence in all of history was committed. A superficial glossing over of the problem of sin would not have sufficed. God had to cut through to its very heart in order to purchase our peace.

> He was pierced for our transgressions,
> he was crushed for our iniquities;
> the punishment that brought us peace was upon him,
> and by his wounds we are healed. [Isa. 53:5]

The price of our peace was enormous.

The Prince of Peace did not come to smooth ruffled feathers. Not at the personal, the national, or the international level. His is a peace that starts in the heart and works its way outward, never the other way around. That is why it is a peace that "transcends all understanding." The people around us look at the superficial circumstances that surround us. They can't understand what is going on in the heart of a child of God. Human understanding would have us believe that peace must work from the outside in.

The word *shalom* is even today used as a greeting by the Jewish people. The apostle Paul used it as a greeting and closing in most of his letters. Jesus greeted his dear friends, "Peace I leave with you; my peace I give you. . . ." And Jesus said, "Peace be with you" as he appeared to his assembled disciples after his death and resurrection (Luke 24:36). But when Jesus, Prince of Peace, uses the greeting *shalom*, it is far more than an intangible greeting or a wish. It is a gift. It is the gift of the Person who himself is peace.

I am who you need. I am your perfection. I am your

117

completeness. I am your reconciliation. I am your peace—this is the message of Jesus Christ, Prince of Peace.

The God of peace is still engaged in less than tranquil activity, and we are still confronted with less than tranquil circumstances. But the price of our peace has already been paid. The promised Peace who has begun to work in the hearts of the children of God will, one day, work his way outward. The result will be that men will beat their swords into plowshares, and the lion will lie down with the lamb.

> May the God of peace, who through the blood of the eternal covenant brought back from the dead our Lord Jesus, that great Shepherd of the sheep, equip you with everything good for doing his will, and may he work in us what is pleasing to him, through Jesus Christ, to whom be glory for ever and ever. Amen. [Heb. 13:20]

"Peace be with you."
"And with you."*

---

*If you are using this with a group, it might be meaningful to "pass the peace" around your group. Each person says to the next, "Peace be with you." The person addressed responds, "And with you," until this greeting has gone all around the group.

118

# 37

## Living Bread

**Scripture:** John 6:1–14, 25–59;
1 Corinthians 11:23–24

Then Jesus declared, "I am the bread of life. He
who comes to me will never go hungry. . . ."
[John 6:35a]

"I am the *living bread* that came down from
heaven. If a man eats of this bread, he will live
forever. This bread is my flesh, which I will give
for the life of the world." [John 6:51]

The Lord Jesus, on the night he was betrayed,
took bread, and when he had given thanks, he
broke it and said, "This is my body, which is for
you; do this in remembrance of me." [1 Cor.
11:23–24]

B read has been referred to as the staff of
life. It is symbolic of the food we need for sustenance—not an optional food, like pickles, artichokes,
or chocolate. Bread is what supports us, nourishes us,

119

and keeps us alive. The fragrance of freshly baked bread is an unspoken invitation few can resist.

In the late eighteenth century, the queen of France, Marie Antoinette, became notorious for her extravagant lifestyle at a time when her government was facing financial crises. She is said to have one day asked an official why the Parisians were angry.

"They are hungry, and have no bread," was the reply.

She has been remembered throughout two centuries for the insensitive response attributed to her: "Let them eat cake." Nourishment, not just something to fill them up, was what the French people needed.

What a contrast this attitude is to the one shown by Jesus (John 6)! A great crowd had followed Jesus around the Sea of Galilee to see the miracles he was doing and to hear his teaching. There were no roadside fast-food restaurants for these people who had walked quite a distance from their homes.

"How shall we feed these people?" Jesus asked his disciples.

"You've got to be kidding," they responded. "We could spend eight months' salary and we would not have given everyone in this crowd even a bite of bread."

One boy had thought ahead (or perhaps his mother had). He had brought a small lunch with him. Not much. But in the hands of the One who is the living Bread that small lunch provided an ample meal for well over five thousand people, with twelve baskets of leftovers.

"I am the bread of life," Jesus said later to some of the people who thought they had located a permanent free lunch ticket. Many didn't understand. They would be hungry again for the kind of food that spoils. But Jesus himself could supply them the kind of nourishment that would permanently quiet the spiritual hunger pangs each one had within himself. Just as men need bread for nourishment in order to live, so they need the sustenance Jesus supplies in order to live eternally.

A loaf of bread, golden brown and still warm from the oven, looks beautiful. But in order to do any good for anyone, it must be broken—first with hands or knife, then with teeth. Finally, the body's digestive juices continue the "breaking down" process, in order that the bread may do what it was meant to do.

Jesus, the living Bread, also had to be broken in order to do what he was meant to do—be life for us. What Jesus offers is not cake—sweet, temporarily filling, but not particularly nourishing. Jesus offers bread—something both desirable and good for us. He offers to be for us what we need to live. He himself is the staff of life—eternal life.

# 38

## The Word

**Scripture:** John 1:1–18; Revelation
19:11–16

In the beginning was *the Word*, and the Word
was with God, and the Word was God. He was
with God in the beginning. [John 1:1–2]

The Word became flesh and made his dwelling
among us. We have seen his glory, the glory of
the One and Only, who came from the Father,
full of grace and truth. [John 1:14]

He is dressed in a robe dipped in blood, and his
name is the Word of God. [Rev. 19:13]

Friends of a young man had told him about
a girl they thought he should meet. They showed him
a picture of her. He was interested, but many miles
separated them. How could he get to know her at
such a distance? He sent her a letter, telling her in
his own words who he was, what he valued, what his
goals were. And she wrote back. The young man's

most effective means of communicating what he was like was his word.

God has given us the testimony of friends. God has given us pictures—think of some of the names we have considered: bread, door, star, lamb, vine. But his most effective expression of who he himself is, is his Word, Jesus Christ.

The right word enhances our understanding. It strips away the fog that surrounds a difficult or abstract concept. It can cut through a broad generality, making it clear that the speaker means A, not B or C.

The right word, from the right person, can be all that is necessary to establish credibility. "Give me your word, and I'll believe it."

The word is a reflection of what is in the heart. "Out of the overflow of [the] heart [the] mouth speaks," says Luke (6:45). The living Word was with God, and was God from the beginning. He is the overflow of the abundant love which is the essence of the heart of God.

The living Word is God's best expression of himself. The Word clarifies who God is for us and enhances our understanding of him. The living Word is the best evidence for God's credibility.

Think of the power an ordinary word has in certain contexts: a jury foreman announces guilty; a young girl replies yes; the umpire calls strike; a congress declares war. The power of the living Word far exceeds the power of any other word. We need not fear a world filled with devils, or the rage of the prince of darkness, for "one little Word shall fell him."

> That Word above all earthly powers,
> No thanks to them, abideth;

123

The Spirit and the gifts are ours
  Through him who with us sideth;
Let goods and kindred go,
  This mortal life also;
The body they may kill:
  God's truth abideth still;
His kingdom is forever.

—Martin Luther, 1529

A word, once spoken, cannot be unsaid. God has expressed himself in the incarnate Word. He cannot and will not reverse himself. That Word is with us forever.

Come, thou Incarnate Word,
Gird on thy mighty sword,
Our prayer attend:
Come and thy people bless,
And give thy Word success. . . . Amen.

—Anonymous, c. 1757

# 39

## Rose of Sharon
**Scripture:** Song of Solomon 2:1

I am a *rose of Sharon*,
a lily of the valleys. [Song of Sol. 2:1]

The rose of Sharon is a large hibiscus shrub. It grows about twelve feet tall, has large three-lobed leaves, and a lovely rose, purple, white, or blue flower.

The uniqueness of the rose of Sharon lies in the fact that it blooms at an unlikely time and in unlikely places. The rose blossoms in the fall, when few other shrubs are in bloom. It grows well in unfavorable conditions, and does not seem to be partial to city or country.

Unfavorable growing conditions? In our honest moments we sometimes marvel that the soil of our lives could produce anything beautiful. It is full of the stones of selfishness, the weeds of deceitfulness, and the acidity of our pride. Yet the Rose of Sharon persists, blooms, and grows, even when other plants are dormant.

Jesus, Rose of Sharon, bloom in my heart today. Let the lives of those around me be touched by the beauty and the fragrance of your love. Those who know me will wonder that such poor soil could produce such a flower. They will know that it is the tenacity of the flower, not the quality of the soil, and we will all praise you!

> Lo, how a rose upspringing
> On tender root has grown:
> A rose by prophet's singing
> To all the world made known.
> The Rose 'midst winter's cold
> A lovely blossom bearing,
> In former days foretold.
>
> This Flow'r whose fragrance tender
> With sweetness fills the air,
> Dispels with glorious splendor
> The darkness everywhere.
> True Man, yet very God;
> From sin and death he saves us
> And lightens every load.
>
> —German author, unknown (c. 1500)

# 40

## Holy, Holy, Holy
**Scripture:** Isaiah 6:1–8; Exodus 33:17–23; 1 Peter 1:15–16

*"Holy, holy, holy* is the Lord Almighty;
   the whole earth is full of his glory." [Isa. 6:3]

Day and night they never stop saying:
"Holy, holy, holy
is the Lord God Almighty,
who was, and is, and is to come." [Rev. 4:8b]

In all of Scripture this is the one name or attribute of God that is named three times in succession. The emphasis cannot be accidental. God is so named by the four living creatures in Revelation, and by the seraphim in Isaiah's vision. There are other names of God that are much easier for us to think about. If we are honest, this one makes us a little squeamish.

As we look at this name of God, the nearer we approach, and the more clearly we see, the more uncomfortable we become. To look at God's holiness is something like looking with unshaded eyes directly at the sun. God told Moses that no one could see his face and live. God covered Moses with his hand and allowed him to see his back! Moses' face shone as a result of this encounter.

The early Israelites were so conscious of God's holiness that they would never speak his name aloud, or write it, except in abbreviated form. We, on the other hand, sometimes are so casual that we lose the impact of what it means for the holy, holy, holy God to make himself one with sinful man. No analogy can do justice to the reality of God's incarnation for the purpose of our atonement, but perhaps we can begin to think in the right direction if we imagine a beautifully and carefully made white wedding dress being drenched in the sewer. Or imagine your thirteen-year-old daughter being raped. But because God is God, the sewer and the rape did not ruin him.

Not only is God holy, but he expects us to be holy also (1 Peter 1:15–16). Sometimes it seems more socially acceptable to be a little less than holy. Being holy doesn't always sound like a lot of fun. Sometimes being holy seems like an impossible achievement. It would be, if we had to do it by ourselves!

We have met the holy, holy, holy God. Such an encounter must have one of two results: blasphemy or worship. Isaiah worshiped. In Isaiah 6, he catches a glimpse of the holy God in a service of worship which begins with adoration and praise. Isaiah confesses his sin, and is then assured of God's pardon. The word of the Lord is proclaimed, and Isaiah responds. The outgrowth of his worship is service.

128

Service which does not spring from having worshiped, as Isaiah's did, soon becomes meaningless.

Holy, holy, holy God. Like Isaiah, when we are confronted with your holiness we become more acutely aware of our own sinfulness. We acknowledge it and we confess it. Help us to forsake our sin, to the end that we may obey your command to be holy, even as you are holy.

Holy, holy, holy God in three persons. We are full of wonder that you have made atonement for our sin.

Holy, holy, holy God. With Isaiah, we respond to your word, "Here am I. Send me!"

# 41

## Friend of Tax Collectors and Sinners
**Scripture:** Luke 7:34–50

"The Son of Man came eating and drinking, and they say, 'Here is . . . a *friend of tax collectors and "sinners."'* " [Matt. 11:19]

. . . but there is a friend who sticks closer than a brother. [Prov. 18:24]

"Greater love has no one than this, that he lay down his life for his friends." [John 15:13]

Even more hated than the Roman conquerors were the tax collectors. The tax collector was no foreigner. He might have had a farm just down the road. He might have been Uncle Ezra's second cousin. A greedy tax collector (and most of them were) could demand not only the revenue required by Rome, but also an additional amount to line his own pockets. He could get away with this, because he was backed by Roman soldiers, who could, if necessary, be very persuasive! Such a collector turned his back on his friends in exchange for cash and clout.

Yet as Jesus was passing through Jericho one day, it was a tax collector he singled out from the crowd. It was a tax collector with whom Jesus chose to have lunch. As a result of Jesus' gracious friendship, Zacchaeus the tax collector became a changed man (Luke 19).

Matthew, another tax collector, was chosen to be part of Jesus' inner circle. He was one of the twelve who walked, worked, watched, ate, slept, and lived with Jesus during his time of ministry on earth. This collector of taxes later used his recordkeeping ability to become a chronicler of the life of Jesus, his friend.

In a culture which didn't view any woman very highly, Jesus befriended "used" women. One prostitute was overwhelmed by the compassion she had experienced and the forgiveness she knew she had received from God. This broken woman poured on Jesus' feet her tears of repentance, together with the costly perfume from her broken jar (Luke 7). She had been made whole.

Then there was the foreign woman who slept around. She came to the well for her daily water supply at a time when none of the other women would be there, probably because they would look down their noses at her. Jesus befriended this woman, as well. She became a new person (John 4).

Fellow friends of Jesus! Look around you at the company we are in! Prostitutes, cheats, liars—Jesus even called Judas his friend (Matt. 26:50). Just as there is nothing we ourselves can do to be worthy of his friendship, so there is nothing we can do to make ourselves ineligible for it.

The friendship has been offered. Jesus has extended his nail-scarred hand to us. All we need do is take it, and like the tax collectors and sinners before us, we won't ever be the same!

Today, let us

> Ponder anew what the Almighty will do,
> If with his love he befriend thee!

> —Joachim Neander, 1680

# 42

## Omega
**Scripture:** Psalm 102:25–28; Psalm 46

"I am . . . the *Omega*, . . . the Last, . . . the End."
[Rev. 22:13]

But you [God] remain the same,
and your years will never end. [Ps. 102:27]

S o much of that with which we involve
ourselves has an end. We spend ourselves preparing
for a special visitor or a special occasion. The visit
always ends and the occasion is soon over. Time itself
has an end. But God? Why does our eternal God name
himself with the last letter of the Greek alphabet,
omega? What can the name *Omega* tell us about
God?

Sometimes advertisers use the phrase *the last word
in* . . . [whatever they are trying to sell]. They wish
to convey the idea that after we have investigated
every other similar product, we will find this one to
be superior. Nothing else can surpass it.

Sometimes someone is said to have had "the last word" in a discussion or debate. The idea is that after everyone else has had his say and has presented his best argument, this one's word prevailed.

Omega God, nothing and no one will ever surpass you! Omega God, when all other words have been spoken, your Word prevails!

What does it mean to belong to the Omega God? What does it mean to be part of the unending ending? C. S. Lewis gives us a hint as he concludes the last of his chronicles of Narnia:

> For us this is the end of all the stories, and we can most truly say that they all lived happily ever after. But for them it was only the beginning of the real story. All their life in this world and all their adventures in Narnia had only been the cover and the title page: now at last they were beginning Chapter One of the Great Story, which no one on earth has read: which goes on for ever: in which every chapter is better than the one before.*

Man's chief end is to glorify God and to enjoy him *forever*, says the Westminster Catechism. Are we so immersed in today that we never stop to think about what our worshiping will be like in 100 years? Or what it will be like in 1,000 years? Or, how about 479,502 years from now?

Belonging to the Omega God means that our worship takes on eternal significance. Our task of inviting others to worship—our families, our neighbors, those with whom we work—takes on eternal signifi-

*C. S. Lewis, *The Last Battle* (New York: Macmillan, 1956), p. 184.

cance. And our task of equipping ourselves and others to be better worshipers is eternally significant.

Help us, Omega God—you who precede all beginnings and succeed all endings—help us to look beyond the needs and demands of today. Equip us to better worship you, Omega God, the Last, the everlasting One.

# Appendix
## Join All the Glorious Names!

This is a listing, in alphabetical order, of names of God and Scripture passages where they are found. The names are from the New International Version, unless otherwise noted.

I am indebted to Virgil and Carol Olson of Pasadena, California, for their assistance in compiling this list.

**Abba** Romans 8:15
**Advocate** 1 John 2:1 (KJV)
**Almighty** Psalm 68:14
**Alpha** Revelation 22:13
**Amen** Revelation 3:14
**Ancient of Days** Daniel 7:9
**Anointed One** Psalm 2:2
**Apostle and High Priest** Hebrews 3:1
**Arm of the Lord** Isaiah 53:1
**Author of Life** Acts 3:15
**Author of Our Faith** Hebrews 12:2

**Beginning and the End** Revelation 21:6
**Blessed and Only Ruler** 1 Timothy 6:15
**Branch** Jeremiah 33:15
**Bread of God** John 6:33
**Bread of Life** John 6:35
**Bridegroom** Isaiah 62:5b
**Bright Morning Star** Revelation 22:16
**Chief Shepherd** 1 Peter 5:4
**Chosen One** Isaiah 42:1
**Christ** Matthew 22:42

136

**Christ of God** Luke 9:20
**Christ the Lord** Luke 2:11
**Christ, the Son of the Living God** Matthew 16:16
**Comforter** John 14:26 (KJV)
**Commander** Isaiah 55:4
**Consolation of Israel** Luke 2:25
**Consuming Fire** Deuteronomy 4:24; Hebrews 12:29
**Cornerstone** Isaiah 28:16
**Counselor** John 14:26
**Creator** 1 Peter 4:19
**Deliverer** Romans 11:26
**Desired of All Nations** Haggai 2:7
**Door** John 10:7 (KJV)
**El Shaddai** Genesis 17:1 (Hebrew)
**Eternal God** Deuteronomy 33:27
**Everlasting Father** Isaiah 9:6
**Exact Representation of His [God's] Being** Hebrews 1:3
**Faithful and True** Revelation 19:11
**Faithful Witness** Revelation 1:5
**Father** Matthew 6:9
**Firstborn among Many Brothers** Romans 8:29
**Firstborn from the Dead** Revelation 1:5
**Firstborn over All Creation** Colossians 1:15
**Firstfruits** 1 Corinthians 15:20, 23
**Foundation** 1 Corinthians 3:11
**Friend of Tax Collectors and "Sinners"** Matthew 11:19
**Gentle Whisper** 1 Kings 19:12
**Gift of God** John 4:10
**Glory of the Lord** Isaiah 40:5
**God** Genesis 1:1
**God Almighty** Genesis 17:1

**God over All** Romans 9:5
**God Who Sees Me** Genesis 16:13
**Good Shepherd** John 10:11
**Great High Priest** Hebrews 4:14
**Great Shepherd** Hebrews 13:20
**Guide** Psalm 48:14
**Head of the Body** Colossians 1:18
**Head of the Church** Ephesians 5:23
**Heir of All Things** Hebrews 1:2
**High Priest Forever** Hebrews 6:20
**Holy One** Acts 2:27
**Holy One of Israel** Isaiah 49:7
**Holy Spirit** John 14:26
**Hope** Titus 2:13
**Horn of Salvation** Luke 1:69
**I Am** Exodus 3:14; John 8:58
**Image of God** 2 Corinthians 4:4
**Image of His Person** Hebrews 1:3 (KJV)
**Immanuel** Isaiah 7:14
**Jehovah** Psalm 83:18 (KJV)
**Jesus** Matthew 1:21
**Jesus Christ Our Lord** Romans 6:23
**Judge** Isaiah 33:22; Acts 10:42
**King** Zechariah 9:9
**King Eternal** 1 Timothy 1:17
**King of Kings** 1 Timothy 6:15
**King of the Ages** Revelation 15:3
**Lamb of God** John 1:29
**Last Adam** 1 Corinthians 15:45
**Lawgiver** Isaiah 33:22
**Leader** Isaiah 55:4
**Life** John 14:6
**Light of the World** John 8:12
**Like an Eagle** Deuteronomy 32:11
**Lily of the Valleys** Song of Solomon 2:1
**Lion of the Tribe of Judah** Revelation 5:5

137

Living Stone 1 Peter 2:4
Living Water John 4:10
Lord John 13:13
Lord God Almighty Revelation 15:3
Lord Jesus Christ 1 Corinthians 15:57
Lord of All Acts 10:36
Lord of Glory 1 Corinthians 2:8
Lord of Lords 1 Timothy 6:15
Lord Our Righteousness Jeremiah 23:6
Love 1 John 4:8
Man of Sorrows Isaiah 53:3
Master Luke 5:5
Mediator 1 Timothy 2:5
Merciful God Jeremiah 3:12b
Messenger of the Covenant Malachi 3:1
Messiah John 4:25
Mighty God Isaiah 9:6
Mighty One Isaiah 60:16
Nazarene Matthew 2:23
Offspring of David Revelation 22:16
Omega Revelation 22:13
Only Begotten Son John 1:18 (KJV)
Our Passover Lamb 1 Corinthians 5:7
Our Peace Ephesians 2:14
Potter Isaiah 64:8b
Power of God 1 Corinthians 1:24
Prince of Peace Isaiah 9:6
Prophet Acts 3:22
Purifier Malachi 3:3
Rabboni (Teacher) John 20:16
Radiance of God's Glory Hebrews 1:3
Redeemer Job 19:25
Refiner's Fire Malachi 3:2
Resurrection and the Life John 11:25

Righteous One 1 John 2:1
Rock 1 Corinthians 10:4
Root of David Revelation 22:16
Rose of Sharon Song of Solomon 2:1
Ruler of God's Creation Revelation 3:14
Ruler of the Kings of the Earth Revelation 1:5
Ruler over Israel Micah 5:2
Savior Luke 2:11
Scepter Out of Israel Numbers 24:17
Seed Genesis 3:15
Servant Isaiah 42:1
Shepherd and Overseer of Your Souls 1 Peter 2:25
Shield Genesis 15:1
Son of David Matthew 1:1
Son of God Matthew 27:54
Son of Man Matthew 8:20
Son of the Most High Luke 1:32
Source of Eternal Salvation Hebrews 5:9
Spirit of God Genesis 1:2
Star Out of Jacob Numbers 24:17
Stone 1 Peter 2:8
Sun of Righteousness Malachi 4:2
Teacher John 13:13
True Light John 1:9
True Witness Revelation 3:14
Truth John 14:6
Vine John 15:5
Way John 14:6
Wisdom of God 1 Corinthians 1:24
Witness Isaiah 55:4
Wonderful Counselor Isaiah 9:6
Word John 1:1
Word of God Revelation 19:13